WILTSHIRE TOLL HOUSES

Devizes (Shane's Castle)

Wiltshire Toll Houses

Robert Haynes
and Ivor Slocombe

First published in the United Kingdom in 2004 by
The Hobnob Press, PO Box 1838, East Knoyle, Salisbury SP3 6FA

This book has been published with the generous help of a grant from the Wiltshire Branch of the Royal Institute of British Architects. Proceeds from sales will go to the funds of the Wiltshire Buildings Record.

British Library Cataloguing in Publication Data
A catalogue record for this book is available from the British Library.

ISBN 0-946418-21-7

Typeset in 11/13.5 pt Scala
Typesetting and origination by John Chandler
Printed in Great Britain by Salisbury Printing Company Ltd, Salisbury

Preface

THE INSPIRATION for and much of the content of this book come from Robert (Bob) Haynes. Bob was an architect who spent most of his working life in local government. After periods in Hertfordshire, Devon and Buckinghamshire, he came to Wiltshire in 1966 as Deputy County Architect becoming County Architect in 1980. He was a man of wide interests and great enthusiasm and, after his retirement in 1986, he was able to devote much of his time to developing the work he had previously started. But his greatest passion was for milestones, recording and photographing the many remaining examples in the county. From this, especially with his architectural background, it was natural to move on to a study of toll houses. He left a large amount of material, particularly illustrations, on both existing toll houses and those which have disappeared in recent years.

It has been my task to prepare his material for publication. I have been able to supplement his efforts with more research on the documentary evidence which helps to give a background to the construction of toll houses and, in many cases, their demise.

This book has several aims. First, it provides as complete a gazetteer as possible of all known toll houses in the county whether still standing or demolished. Second, it attempts to draw together the evidence from individual toll houses to give an overview of their design and form, their construction and the factors which led to their particular siting. Finally, it reminds us that toll houses should be seen not in isolation but as an integral part of the turnpike system which dominated the history of roads in this country for well over a century.

Ivor Slocombe

Acknowledgements

WE ARE GRATEFUL to the occupants of various toll houses for their ready agreement for their houses to be studied and photographed. We are also grateful for the help of many individuals and organisations including; Geoffrey Crowe, John Chandler, Ruth Newman, Roger Mawby, Michael Marshman, Hilary Dunscombe, Alan Thomsett, the Cricklade Historical Society, Alyson Curtis, Rosalind Pasmore, Christine Lombard, Highworth History Society, Peter Brown. Over the years much assistance has been given too by the Wiltshire and Swindon Record Office, the W.C.C. Local Studies Library and by the Wiltshire Buildings Record.

Please respect the privacy of the occupants of the toll houses.

Introduction

AN ESSENTIAL FEATURE of the turnpike roads was the toll gates and their associated toll houses. It might be expected, perhaps, that the pattern of gates and houses was set when each turnpike was established mainly in the mid 18th century and that little change occurred after that. Also, each turnpike trust had its own standard design for its milestones and it would have been logical to follow a similar policy in its plans for the toll houses. In practice, however, there was a tremendous variation and frequent change. The sites of the gates were often reviewed and moved to more effective positions with a consequent impact on the toll houses. Although it is possible to find some similarity amongst toll houses, for example within the Amesbury Trust and within the Bradford Trust, there was from the start a range of plans, sizes and styles. Many of the Trusts seem to have undertaken a significant re-building of toll houses in the mid 19th century, only 30 or 40 years before the closure of the turnpikes, and these later toll houses tend to be grander and designed in keeping with current architectural fashions.

Toll booths

It is almost certain that each gate had some kind of provision for the toll collector. At the minor gates, and especially at the toll bars controlling side roads, this was little more than a small booth. Naturally these have disappeared but the old photograph of Winsley (Turleigh) shows such a wooden booth. The records of the Bradford Trust, which included Turleigh, refer in 1838 to an order for two booths 'of the proper dimensions . . . and made properly of Keanized timber.' This was timber saturated with Keyans patent solution, an early wood preservative. At Grittleton (Jockey) the Trust had to give up its lease of its toll house and decided to replace it with a toll booth 'to be built at the least expense'. Again this was to be of timber although it did have an iron stove. A slightly more substantial provision was made by the Salisbury and Eling Trust on the top of

Three Mile Hill, 'a brick shed about seven feet square and seven feet high with a slate covering ... and a proper toll board on the building'.

Small Toll Houses

A toll house had essentially to be functional. It needed to be close to the roadside and turnpike gate; it would benefit from having clear visibility of the road in both directions; a central door would give easy access to the gate; and a suitable wall was required on which to affix the board with the list of tolls. The house could be of one or two storeys but the living accommodation would be only modest befitting the rather lowly occupation of toll collector. Many toll houses had only the one front door with no access from the rear. It has been suggested that this was perhaps for reasons of security considering the amount of cash which must have been kept in the house.

The Swindon toll houses (Rushey Platt, Regent Street and Cricklade Road) were the most modest of buildings being of one storey, probably only two rooms and under a thatched roof. The Purton (Collins Lane) house represents what most would regard as the 'typical' toll house. Of two storeys, it has a projecting bay with windows angled to the road, a central door and, above it, a blank wall on which the toll board is fixed.

The nature of these small toll houses can also be judged from their building costs. The Salisbury and Eling Trust, for example, ordered on its establishment in 1753 the erection of three toll houses at St. Thomas' Bridge, Petersfinger and Eling. The cost of each was not to exceed £30. The Westbury Trust had a contract in 1786 with John Elkins, a carpenter, to build a toll house in Warminster Lane for £27 16s. These houses are at the lowest end of the scale but a cost of around £60 seems to have been most common for these early toll houses. The bill from Mr. Wicks for building the toll house at Marsh Gate, Swindon, 'a substantial building of stone, slate, timber and all proper materials', was £61. At a rather later date, 1839, the Bradford Trust adopted three different plans: they built one on Plan 1 at a cost of £86, two on Plan 2 at £90 and £94, and two on Plan 3 at £100 and £115.

Use of Existing Houses

Instead of erecting a completely new toll house, Trusts sometimes made use of existing buildings. This could be by buying or renting a convenient house, often then appointing the sitting tenant as toll collector. Alternatively the Trust might extend an existing terrace of cottages.

At Calne (Mile Elm), for example, the Calne Trust in 1859 bought two cottages and converted them into a toll house. At Bradford the Trust rented a house in St. Margaret's Street from Mrs. Deverell for 10 guineas a year. Often it was the turnpike gate which was moved in order to be near a convenient house. This seems to have been of some value to the owner of the house as is shown in the movement in 1767 of the gate across the road from Melksham to the Forest. It was agreed that the gate would be moved to a house belonging to John Prutty and occupied by Jacob Wilshere and his wife, Mary, who were then appointed the toll collectors. For this 'privilege' John Prutty had to meet the cost of moving the gate and to do so within 14 days otherwise the agreement would be void. The lack of security of tenure which went with leasing could cause problems for the Trust. At Grittleton (Jockey) the Trust had rented a cottage from the Neeld family but in 1850 John Neeld asked for and obtained repossession of the house. The Trust then had to make other arrangements, eventually settling on the cheapest alternative, a wooden hut.

There are other examples where a toll house had been clearly built on to a row of older cottages. At Chiseldon (Turnball) the original row of stone cottages appears to be of the 17th century. A toll house of stone was built and a brick front was added probably in the early 19th century. At Upton Scudamore the newer toll house is clearly visible, being several feet higher than its linked cottages.

Larger Toll Houses

Some toll houses were built on a larger scale although these tend to be of rather later date. The Dilton Marsh (Clivey) house, for example, built in the early 19th century was quite substantial even without the later additions. On a similar scale was the Box (Kingsdown) house also of the early 19th century. The Wilton Trust adopted a similar policy in replacing the toll house at Fisherton Anger. The scale of the house is indicated by the fact that it cost nearly £400 to build. Other Trusts resisted the temptation to spend lavishly. The Sarum and Eling Trust, for example, in 1833 rejected an elaborate plan for the Winterslow (Lopcombe Corner) house in favour of a much less expensive one.

The grandest houses, however, resulted from the major rebuilding programme of the Trowbridge Trust in the 1840s. Although the Stallard and Polebarn houses are now demolished, the old photographs show houses which bear no resemblance to those early, modest toll houses. It was, in fact, the decision to build such houses which led to the premature closure of the turnpike. The Trust had until 1877 to run but in 1869 there was a successful petition to the House of Commons Committee to rescind the Trust. The main cause of complaint was that the Trust, instead of using its income to pay off outstanding debts and loans, had squandered its money on building new, large toll houses, including Stallard. The turnpike was said to have 12 main toll houses in a stretch of 35 miles.

Architect Designed Toll Houses

Most of the smaller toll houses were vernacular buildings i.e. of local materials and designed and built by a local mason or carpenter. But some were clearly architect-designed, perhaps emulating or at least influenced by the lodges of the greater houses of Wiltshire.

The ornate, thatched toll houses at Aldbourne, Trowbridge (The Down) and Warminster (Henfords Marsh) certainly fall into this category. In a similar vein is the 'Strawberry Hill Gothick' of the Mildenhall (Savernake) toll house which seems to have become an estate lodge when it was sold in 1871. The castellated Shane's Castle holds a prominent position on the entrance to Devizes but it may not be unique. There is a reference to another castellated toll house at Trowbridge (Studley) although this one has been long demolished.

The old photograph of Devizes (The Green) shows an impressive classical portico although the architect is not known. There is some evidence that the Salisbury architect John Peniston did some work for various Trusts. He seems to have made three drawings for the proposed Fisherton Anger toll house but none of these was adopted. His letters suggest that perhaps he was more involved with survey work and inspecting newly built houses.

Movement of Toll Houses

The movement of the toll house in Warminster to a new site in Boreham Road has been well documented. The house built in East Street in 1828 was taken down in 1840 and re-erected using the same materials and on the same plan. It was assumed that this case was unique but there at least two other examples in Wiltshire.

The Bradford Trust reorganised its gates in 1839 and, as part of this, built a new toll house at Dainton's Grave. Two years later, for a reason which is not apparent, the house was taken down and re-built on its present site on the road to Westwood.

The Wroughton example is rather different. The Trust in 1857 built a new toll house at Wharf Road in the centre of the village but this was very unpopular with the local inhabitants. After some difficult negotiations it was agreed that the toll house should be moved further up the hill but the village had to meet the cost of moving the materials.

It might be asked why a Trust should decide to move a toll house in this way rather than simply selling the old house and erecting a new one. It can only be assumed that it was cheaper to do so and there is some evidence to support this. In the Bradford case, the toll house cost £115 to build but only £26 to take down and re-erect. This indicates that the materials were valuable and constituted a very high proportion of the cost compared with the labour. Also, at the end of the turnpikes, toll houses were sold off at prices considerably lower than they had cost to build. That might be a special circumstance but it may indicate that the market for the sale of houses was not a buoyant one. A combination of those two factors would make it more economic to move and re-erect a toll house.

Appurtenances

Toll houses needed to have certain appurtenances although the scope of the Trust was limited by the Act which created the turnpike. The most important provision was a garden. This was sometimes made difficult by the site of the toll house, for example in the fork of two joining roads. In such cases a detached garden, if necessary on the opposite of the road, was provided as at Devizes (Shane's Castle), Chilmark and Gomeldon. The total size of the plot might vary but was never very large: 11 perches at Milford (Lopcombe) but only 3 perches at Gomeldon and Hilperton.

Later sale particulars also refer to outbuildings and washhouses. At the Seend gate house a cellar under the sitting room was used as a wash house. In 1846 this was improved by installing a water supply, putting in a drain to take away the refuse water and making a draught hole on one side and an iron grating on the other to extract steam.

Stables are less frequently mentioned. Those at Poulshot, Trowbridge (Stallard) and Warminster (Boreham Road) may have been used by other turnpike officials rather than by the resident toll collectors.

As many toll houses were quite isolated, attention had to be given to a suitable water supply. Most commonly this was done by the sinking of a well. At Westbury (Warminster Lane) in 1791 the lessee of the tolls was allowed three guineas for making a well near the house and providing a windlass and bucket for it. In 1842 the surveyor was ordered not only to sink a well at the Bradford (Westwood) toll house but also to erect a privy for the use of the gatekeeper 'the present convenience being inadequate'. The Chilmark toll house has long been demolished but the 1926 6" O.S. map still shows a well on the site. There is a reference in 1842 to the pond being repaired at the very isolated Urchfont (Redhorn) house but it is not certain whether this was the source of water for the house or simply a watering place for horses.

Weighing Engines and Weighing Houses

The minutes of the various Trusts contain frequent references to weighing engines and weighing houses. The Turnpike Act of 1741 allowed Trusts to charge tolls according to weight and, in order to be able to implement this, to erect 'any crane, machine or engine which they shall judge proper for the weighing of carts, wagons or other carriages'. Weighing engines must have become a common sight along turnpike roads but surprisingly little is known about them and how they worked. Most were probably something like the modern weighbridge. James Edgell of Frome was advertising such machines in the *Gloucester Journal* in 1774:

> These Engines are of a new Construction, and may be placed where those of the old Construction cannot, a Space of Ground of 15 Feet Square, and four Feet in Depth, being sufficient for erecting one of these. They will weigh from one Pound to nine Tons and upwards, and the Weight used for weighing each Ton is only 14 Pounds. The Scale hangs above Ground in the most convenient Part of the Turnpike or Weighing House, and a Quarter Guinea will turn the Beam. By these Engines a small Parcel of Goods as well as a loaded Carriage may be weighed with Accuracy; and a loaded Carriage is weighed with as much Ease and Expedition as a small Parcel in common Scales.

An alternative model, more like a crane, is described by Webb in his *Story of the King's Highway (1913)*: '. . . not the convenient modern weighbridge, which had not then been invented, but a huge and complicated structure, rising high over the road, and actually lifting the vehicle and its contents from the ground. One such machine may still be seen *in situ* at Woodbridge, Suffolk, and a weird and incomprehensible structure it is. Its erection was costly, and the expense of keeping men to work it was still greater. It was never very accurate, and was always getting out of order.'

Probably most of the Wiltshire machines were of the weighbridge type although there was still room for local variations. When the weighbridge was to be erected at Upton Lovell in 1819 various proposals were considered and the contract was awarded to Mr. Hopgood (probably a wheelwright) of Salisbury for an engine on the principle of the model produced by him. Unfortunately it was not reliable and a new engine had to be erected in 1832. There is a reference in 1830 to the sinking of a pit for a new engine in St. Margaret's Street, Bradford which tends to suggest the weighbridge type. Several Trusts employed Mr. Cockey of Frome to design and build their engines and there is also a mention of George Taylor, an engineer, of Bath. The weighing engines must have been capable of being moved as, for example, at Avebury when after the erection of a new model at Beckhampton the old engine was moved to the Kennet gate. Warminster had a weighing engine at least by 1838. It is then shown as being in West Street (now Vicarage Street) close to the junction with Back Street (now Emwell Street). Later it may have been moved to Emwell Street opposite the Weymouth Arms. A weighbridge continued on this site until 1943 when it was destroyed by a tank.

The weighing house contained the mechanism upon which the weights were placed as described in Edgell's advertisement. One such house still stands at Upton Lovell, opposite the toll house. There is also the old photograph of the weighing house at Christ Church, Bradford but this was erected there after the closure of the turnpike. An insight is also given in the minutes of the Wilton Trust in 1830 when alterations were authorised to the weighing house at Salisbury (Fisherton Anger) as it was apparently blocking the footpath for pedestrians.

Loss of Toll Houses

Most of the Turnpike Trusts were closed in the 1870s. Although they had improved the main roads very considerably the payment of tolls was always unpopular. Their closure was consequently marked by great celebrations and firework displays in a number of places including Devizes.

There were probably over 200 toll houses or booths in existence in Wiltshire on the closure of the turnpikes but now only 50 remain. The others have been demolished for a variety of reasons at different periods.

Many of the modest buildings must have proved just unsuitable for modern requirements and gradually fallen into disrepair and then collapse. The Keevil (Strand) toll house is a good example being occupied into the

1950s, then left empty and gradually robbed of its stone roof and other building material.

Other toll houses have had to make way for road improvements. They have been particularly vulnerable being close to the road and often at important road junctions thus making visibility difficult for modern traffic. Trowbridge (Stallard and Polebarn), Avebury (Beckhampton), Roundway (Nursteed) and Warminster (Copheap) have all been such victims in relatively recent times.

But a surprising number of toll houses were demolished on the turnpikes in the 1870s. The Trusts were required to realise their assets to pay off debts, loans and mortgages. The Act stipulated that toll houses should first be offered for sale to the adjoining landowners. Many were disposed of in this way and, perhaps because of the sale restrictions, the purchasers got a bargain. At Beckhampton the new toll house which had cost £109 to build in 1857 was sold in 1870 for £50. The Warminster (Boreham Road) house cost £300 to build in 1828, then £116 to move in 1840. It was sold in 1870 for only £170. Similarly the Warminster (Henfords Marsh) toll house cost £97 in 1840 but thirty years later realised only £50. But, if the landowners declined to buy, their permission was still needed to sell the toll house by public auction. This was sometimes given but, if not, the house had to be demolished and the building materials sold. This happened, for example, at Devizes (The Green), Wroughton (Wharf Road/Vicarage), Salisbury (Fisherton Anger) and Preshute.

Finally some toll houses have been so extensively altered and enlarged over the years that it is now quite difficult to identify them positively as toll houses. It may be, therefore, that other toll houses still exist in Wiltshire but are awaiting recognition.

Toll Collectors

The role of the toll collectors merits further study. Although they must have handled a significant amount of money, the occupation of toll collector was traditionally a very lowly one. Webb describes them as 'mere labourers paid a wage of 10 or 12 shillings a week, often unable to read or write and usually incapable of keeping accounts'. There is some evidence from the Wiltshire censuses to support this view of their status. At the three gates in Charlton the wives were the toll collectors and two of the husbands were agricultural labourers and the other a road labourer. The wives of agricultural labourers were also toll collectors at Chippenham (Hungerdown) and Hilmarton. Retired soldiers also appear as toll collectors. In the 1851 census the toll collector at Chippenham (Bath Road) was Thomas Hornsey aged 61 and described as a Chelsea pensioner. It was also said that the last toll collector at Melksham (Semington Lane) was Abram Bolland, a veteran of the Indian Mutiny. At the end of the 18th century the typical wage was 3s. or 3s. 6d. a week although it was rather higher at Calne (Chilvester) at £25 a year.

Yet it is difficult to imagine that toll houses as substantial as Trowbridge (Stallard) and Warminster (Boreham Road) were built for toll collectors who ranked with agricultural labourers. It is also of interest to note that in 1791 the Westbury gates were farmed out individually and the successful bidder for the Warminster Lane gate was the toll collector there, James Leigh of Leigh. But he is described as a labourer and it is difficult to see how a labourer was able to afford the relatively high investment of £89 5s. a year for the tolls.

Listed Toll Houses

Toll houses have become increasingly valued both as interesting buildings and as an important reminder of a significant phase in the history of English roads. Yet, of the 50 toll houses which have now been positively identified as still standing in Wiltshire, only 19 are listed. There may be no immediate threat to those toll houses not listed but, for the future, it is most important that what remains of the turnpike road era should be protected with as much security as possible.

Short Notice.

TO BE SOLD BY AUCTION,

BY

MESSRS. R. & J. DARLEY

In the Exchange Room at the New Hall, Chippenham,

On WEDNESDAY the 29th of June, 1870,

At FIVE o'clock in the Afternoon precisely, subject to such Conditions as will be then produced,

ALL THAT

COTTAGE

GARDEN and BUILDINGS,

Situate near the Railway Viaduct on the Bath Road, and now used as a Toll House on the Chippenham Turnpike Trust, with the Appurtenances.

CHIPPENHAM, June 27th, 1870.

G. NOYES, Printer, Bookseller, and Stationer, CHIPPENHAM.

WILTSHIRE TOLL HOUSES – GAZETTEER

(The toll houses are listed under the modern parish with the name of the gate/toll house in brackets. The houses in italics have now disappeared.)

Aldbourne (South Street)
Swindon and Hungerford Road 1813-1874

SU 265 756 On the A419 Swindon to Hungerford road in the centre of Aldbourne.

Listed Grade II 9/69 No. 8 Turnpike Cottage

The house of whitewashed sarsen rubble with a thatched roof is probably of the 17th-18th century. It is of one storey with an attic and the thatch has been drawn down to form a porch.

Local opinion says this was a toll house and it would be in the right place on the southern road from London and Hungerford. But no positive evidence has been found to identify this as a toll house. Many alterations have taken place over the past 50 years which may have obscured 'toll house' features.
LB

Aldbourne (Preston)
Swindon and Hungerford Road 1813-1874

SU 276 742 On the A419 Swindon to Hungerford road at Preston one mile south of Aldbourne.

Listed Grade II 4/559

This cottage, built about 1814, is of brick and flint, part rendered, and with a thatched roof. It is of one storey with an attic. The centre bay has a canted front projection and door. The roof is carried out to form a wide overhanging walkway supported on twinned slender iron columns.
LB

Amesbury (Salisbury Road)
Swindon, Marlborough and Everleigh Road 1761-1875

SU 158 410 On the A345 Amesbury to Salisbury road on the southern outskirts of Amesbury.

Listed Grade II 11/66

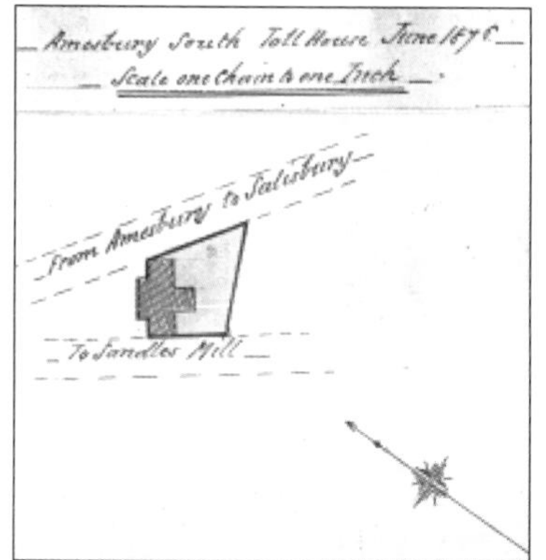

This toll house was built in 1836 on the new turnpike to Old Castle. The unusual appearance of the single storey cottage may have been influenced by the adjacent workhouse (now demolished). It is built of red brick with flint ornamentation and a slate roof. The central section has a single large, round-headed window and the flanking lower wings have similar though smaller windows. The doorway is to the rear. On the closure of the turnpike the toll house was sold in 1878 to Sir Edmund Antrobus for £120.

LB Chandler(Amesbury) TM(Amesbury) WRO A1/205/11

Amesbury (Countess Road)
Amesbury Roads 1761-1871

SU 152 426 On the A345 Amesbury to Marlborough to the north of Amesbury. Listed Grade II 6/37

The toll house was built for the Amesbury Trust in 1762. The red brick two-storey cottage is of square plan with added lean-tos to the rear and north side. It has a projecting porch with a single central window on the upper floor. The tile roof is pyramidal in shape with a chimney stack to the rear. The Trust minutes refer to repairs to the tile roof in 1801-2.
LB Chandler(Amesbury) TM(Amesbury)

Amesbury (West Amesbury)
Amesbury Roads 1761-1871

SU 150 413 On the western outskirts of the town on the road (now unclassified) leading to Stonehenge.

This toll house was probably built in the early days of the Trust and was certainly in existence by 1800. It was similar in design to the Countess and Wylye toll houses. The toll house remained in the ownership of the Trust until its closure in 1871. It was then sold for £70 to Sir Edmund Antrobus.
Chandler(Amesbury) TM(Amesbury) WRO A1/205/2

Atworth (Atworth)
Melksham Roads 1753-1873

ST 862 660 Situated on the north side of the A365 Bath Road.

Listed Grade II 2/15 Turnpike Cottage, 118 Bath Road

The listed buildings register describes this house as a detached single storey cottage with attic, of the 17th century with 18th century additions. It is of rubble stone with stone slate roof and gable end stone stacks. There is a square stone porch with planked door to the left. It is possible, however, that this is the toll house which was built in 1759. In that year the Trust decided to move the gate from Shaw to the Cross Ways in Atworth. They also ordered that a toll house be built there near the dwelling house of Mr. Cox. The toll house is shown on the 1841 Bradford-on-Avon tithe map, the occupier then being Charles Pearce.
LB TM(Box, Seend)

Avebury (Avebury)
Beckhampton Roads 1742-1870

SU 103 700 On the A361 in the centre of the village near the Red Lion Inn.

The evidence from the minutes of the Beckhampton Trust confirms that there was a toll house here although there are few details of the house. It was described as being situated at the corner of the village street leading to Berwick Bassett. In 1804 a weighing engine was moved here from the Beckhampton gate. When the turnpike closed in 1870, the toll house, then occupied by William Collier, was sold to Mr. Peter Neale of the Red Lion Inn for £60.
TM(Beckhampton) WRO A1/205/3

Avebury (Beckhampton, Waggon and Horses)
Beckhampton Roads 1742-1870

SU 090 691 On the A4 Calne to Marlborough road opposite the Waggon and Horses.

Old Toll House. This is a plain brick house, probably of the late 18th century, parallel to the road with a central porch and a window each side. There is a large 20th century extension at the back. The east elevation shows clear signs of the rear of the house being raised. This probably occurred in 1790 for the Trust minutes then refer to the raising of the roof at the back of the house to form a second storey. The outside of the house was then whitewashed. In 1790 the collectors were Stephen Dell and his wife, Mary. In 1804 a new weighing engine was erected at the toll gate by George Taylor, an engineer of Bath, and the old one was repaired and moved to the Kennet gate.

In 1857 it was decided to move the toll gate and erect a new toll house at the Calne-Marlborough/Devizes-Swindon crossroads. In 1870 the turnpike trust was abolished and the old house, then occupied by George Goddard, was bought by Mr. Robert Holford of Westonbirt for £75.
TM(Beckhampton) WRO A1/205/3

Avebury (Beckhampton/Cross roads)
Beckhampton Roads 1742-1870

SU 088 690 On the A4 Calne to Marlborough road at the Beckhampton roundabout.

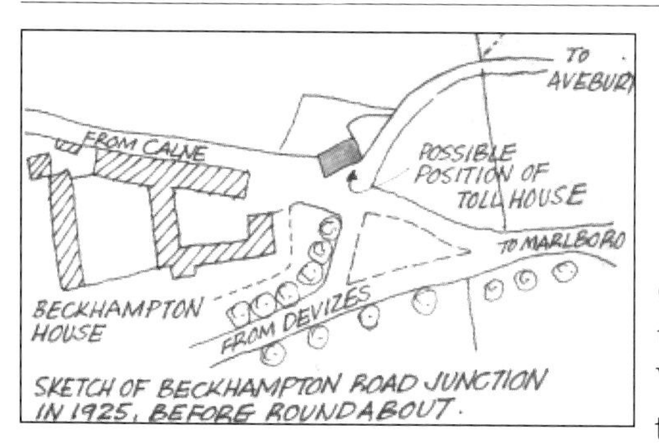

A new toll house was built in 1857 at the Calne–Marlborough/ Devizes–Swindon cross roads to replace the one opposite the Waggon and Horses. In 1870 the house was described as being opposite what used to be the Beckhampton Inn. When the turnpike closed in 1870 the toll house was sold for £50 to Mr. Henry Woolcott, a trainer of race horses at Beckhampton. It is probable that the toll house was demolished to make way for the present roundabout.
TM(Beckhampton) WRO A1/205/3

Avebury (Kennett)
Beckhampton Roads 1742-1870

SU 104 698 Situated on the south east side of the A361 Beckhampton to Swindon road to the south of Avebury on the corner where the main road joins the unclassified road which leads back to the A4.

A toll gate in Avebury was in existence in 1790 when Sarah Tilley, wife of John Tilley, was appointed collector of tolls. In 1797 it was decided to build a toll house 'at the present toll bar leading out of the turnpike road with Avebury Field called Weeden Field.' The land (25 poles) was acquired from Sir Adam Williamson in exchange for land which the Trust had previously purchased from him near Silbury Hill. The Trust also contracted with Sir Adam to erect the toll house for £110. In 1870, with the dissolution of the turnpike, the house was sold to Mr. Richard Jones of Welling, Kent for £75.
TM(Beckhampton) WRO A1/205/3

Biddestone (The Green)
Melksham to Corsham Road 1756-1799

ST 863 736 In the centre of the village at the west side of the Green.

Listed Grade II 9/12 Turnpike Cottage, Church Street.
This cottage, originally a pair, is of the late 18th or early 19th century. It is built of rubble stone with a stone tiled roof and coped north end gable. It has two storeys with one room plan to each cottage. There is a blocked door on the south end elevation. Hinge pins above the door may have supported a board

displaying tolls. In 1993 it still retained a money collecting recess in one front room.
LB

Bishops Cannings (Shepherds Shore)
Beckhampton Roads 1742-1870

SU 045 664 Situated on the west side of the A361 Devizes to Swindon road where it crosses the Wansdyke.

The Beckhampton Trust decided in 1857 to build a new toll house at the Shepherds Shore gate and accepted a tender of £107 from C. E. Pinniger to erect it. When the turnpike ended in 1870 the house was sold to the Commissioner of Woods and Forests for £50. It was then described as adjoining land belonging to Her Majesty and in the occupation of Mr. Sloper.
TM(Beckhampton) WRO A1/205/3

Box (Kingsdown)
Melksham Roads 1753-1873

SU 832 673 On an unclassified road at Blue Vein, west of the cross roads A365/ B3109.

Listed Grade II 2/168

This early 19th century two-storey cottage of hexagonal pattern is ashlar-faced with the other walls of squared rubble stone. It has a projecting porch with a blank window space above, possibly for a toll board. The roof is stone-tiled with a chimney stack offset to one side. There is a 20th century extension at the rear. On the closure of the turnpike in 1870, the toll house was offered to the adjoining landowners, Mr. Northey and Mr. Fuller. They agreed amongst themselves that it should be bought by Mr. Fuller for £50.
LB TM(Lacock Blue Vein)

Box (Melksham Road)
Melksham Roads 1753-1873

SU 827 682 On the A365 Box to Melksham road at the southern edge of Box.

Listed Grade II 3/115 Old Toll House, Devizes Road

This single storey 'Tudor style' cottage of ashlar was built about 1830-40. A projecting central bay contains the doorway and is flanked by mullion windows. It has a slate roof and central chimney stack.
LB

Bradford-on-Avon (Barton Steps)
Bradford-on-Avon Roads 1751-1873

Sale particulars of 1836 for the adjacent 'Chantry' describe that building as 'near the toll gate' but there is no gate shown on the maps of 1774 and 1837. There was certainly a turnpike road along Newtown, running from Winsley through Turleigh to Mason's Hill. There is a reference in 1819 to letting the tolls from the Newtown bar and in the Land Tax records of 1820 the Toll House was owned by Benjamin Hobhouse Esq. and the tenant was E. Williams (probably Ephraim Williams who was a shoemaker in the 1822 Pigot's Directory). On the 1841 tithe map this house was part of plot 137 on the north side of the road opposite Barton Steps. The house was demolished and the site rebuilt in the late 19th century. In 1838 the Trust agreed to make repairs to the toll house in Newtown, the roof being decayed. On the re-organisation of the gates in the Bradford-on-Avon area in 1839, it was agreed to move the Newtown bar to 'the foot of the hill leading into Winsley near the blacksmith's shop'.
TM (Bradford)

Bradford-on-Avon (Cumberwell)
Bradford-on-Avon Roads 1751-1873

The exact position of this toll house at Cumberwell is uncertain. It was probably erected in 1839 following a re-organisation of the gates in the Bradford-on-Avon area. The Trust then accepted a tender from Charles Jones to erect a new toll house at Cumberwell for £94 using the same plan as that for the new house at Widbrook. A year later the Trust entered a contract with Henry Stothert for a new weighing engine at the Cumberwell gate at a cost not exceeding £75.

A further reference occurs in July 1869 when two young men, Daniel Riches and Reginald Fulford, were charged with damaging the toll house at Cumberwell by throwing an eight pound stone at the door, smashing the shutter and eight panes of glass. This was not, however, a planned attack on turnpikes and tolls but simply the young men returning late at night and in high spirits from a fete at Batheaston and doing this for 'a lark to get the old man out to chase us.'
TM(Bradford) SJ(31Jul69)

Bradford-on-Avon (Bradford Leigh)
Bradford-on-Avon Roads 1751-1873

The information available about this toll house is rather sketchy. A map of 1826 shows the Bradford Leigh gate on the Bath road near Leigh House Farm. A toll house certainly existed in 1830 for the Trust then paid a bill for repairing the chimney. In 1839 the turnpike gates in the Bradford-on-Avon area were re-organised with plans for new sites and associated toll houses. Bradford Leigh was one of these and was to be sited 'near the footpath from Woolley to Wraxall'. A tender was received from Charles Jones to build the new toll house at a cost of £108. The Trust then deferred a decision on this in order that the materials from the old Mason's Lane toll house might be used in its erection. There is no further information to confirm whether or not this happened. But in 1841 the Trust received a report that a small window was required in the bedroom of the turnpike house at Bradford Leigh for the purpose of ventilation. Again it is not clear whether this refers to the old toll house or to a new one.
TM(Bradford)

Bradford-on-Avon (Christ Church)
Bradford-on-Avon Roads 1751-1873

Ashmead's map of 1837 shows a toll house in the middle of the junction. It is triangular in plan with a face towards each of the three roads and circular turrets at each angle from which the toll gates radiate. The house must have been demolished some while before the closure of the turnpike in 1873.

The old photograph (date unknown) shows a small octagonal, gothic-style building about 6ft by 6ft by 10ft high. It has traditionally been described as a turnpike weighing engine house but it is not connected with the original toll house.

The turnpike was closed in 1873 and its property put up for sale including the weighing engine and its house at Cumberwell. This had been erected by Henry Stothert in 1840 at a cost of £75. The Town Commissioners considered buying it (they already ran the one in St. Margaret's Street) but decided that it was not desirable to lay out ratepayers' money on this. One of the Commissioners then approached Miss Poynder, a well known local benefactor of Leigh House. She agreed to purchase the engine, to meet all the expenses of removing it and refitting it and then to present it to the town. The engine was bought for £35 but the total cost of the project was estimated to be £100. The work on the engine was done by Messrs. Cockey and Mr. J. Long was employed to do the masonry. The view was expressed that 'the house will be quite an ornament to the neighbourhood where it is to be erected'. It is not certain whether the house was simply re-built or a newly designed house erected.

The photograph must therefore be of the weighing engine house after the engine had been removed and re-erected. It was pulled down in 1931 to make improvements to the road junction.

TM(Bradford) TC(4Jan73, 15Feb73,12Apr73) WT(10Jan1931)

Bradford-on-Avon (St. Margaret's Street)
Bradford-on-Avon Roads 1751-1873

The site of the original toll house is unknown. In 1830 the Trust agreed to rent a house belonging to Mrs. Deverell as the new toll house at a rent of 10 guineas a year. They also erected three gates there and sank a pit for a new weighing engine opposite the house. The house was probably on the west side of St. Margaret's Street just to the north of the junction between Frome Road and Trowbridge Road and part of the gabled cottages demolished in 1935.
TM(Bradford)

Bradford-on-Avon (Westwood)
Bradford-on-Avon Roads 1751-1873

ST 823 597 On the B3109 at the top of Elms Cross Hill near the junction with the road leading to Upper Westwood.

This is a single storey stone cottage with a gabled central projecting bay. The central doorway has been converted to a window. There are modern extensions to the rear. A new toll house was built at Dainton's Grave in 1839 at a cost of £115 as part of the major re-siting of the Bradford gates. In 1841 it was decided to move this house to the top of Elms Cross Hill. As this was undertaken by William Long for only £26, it suggests that the material of the toll house was re-used.
TM(Bradford)

Bradford-on-Avon (Widbrook)
Bradford-on-Avon Roads 1751-1873

ST 835 595 On the A363 Bradford-on-Avon to Trowbridge road opposite Widbrook Farm.

The two-storey stone built house has a tiled roof with a slightly projecting central section of two bays. The doorway to the road has been converted to a window. The sites of the Bradford gates were changed in 1839 and, where necessary, new toll houses were built. The Widbrook toll house was part of this re-building and was erected by Charles Jones at a cost of £90. Possibly the original toll house was only one storey and the second storey was added later. *TM(Bradford)*

Bratton (White Horse)
Westbury Roads 1757-1872

SU 912 523 26 Westbury Road. On the B3098 Westbury to Lavington road at Bratton.

The toll house stands at the junction of the B3098 with an unclassified road which leads up to the White Horse. A turnpike gate is shown in this

position on the 1773 map. Very little is known about its history but there is a reference in the Trust minutes to repairs being done to the Bratton toll house in 1791.
TM(Westbury)

Brinkworth (Grittenham)
Malmesbury and Wootton Bassett Roads 1809-1876

SU 017 826 On the unclassified road from Grittenham to Dauntsey near Strange's Farm.

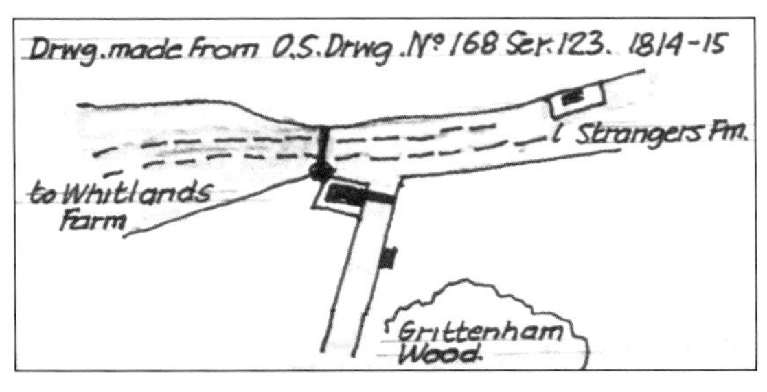

The Victoria County History (Vol. IV) lists the Malmesbury and Wootton Bassett Roads but does not show a branch of the turnpike going through Hooker's Gate and Grittenham towards Dauntsey. However, the Ordnance Surveyor's notes no.168 ser.123 (1814-15) clearly show the conventional sign to denote tollhouses and barriers at both Hooker's Gate and Grittenham.

Broad Hinton (Broad Hinton)
Wootton Bassett and Marlborough Roads 1809-1876

SU 104 767 On the B4041 in the centre of Broad Hinton.

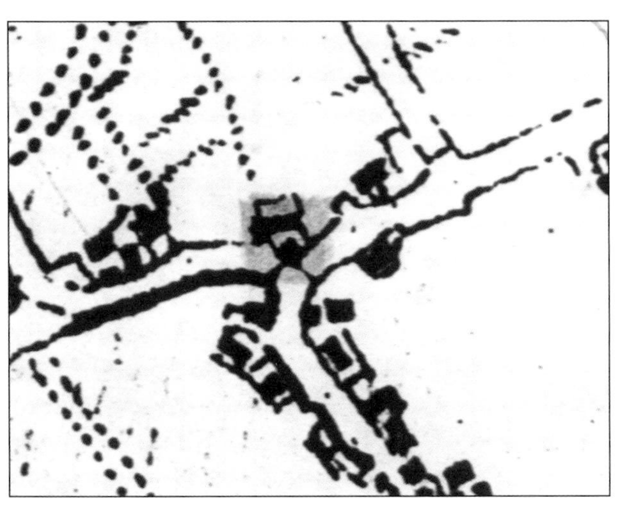

The Ordnance Surveyor's drawings no.168 Ser.123 (1814-15) show toll gates and a tollhouse in the centre of the village, near the later school, on the junction of the B4041 and the unclassified road from The Weir.

Burbage (Ram Alley)

Swindon, Marlborough and Everleigh Road 1761-1875

SU 225 633 On A346 Marlborough to Salisbury road two miles north of Burbage and just south of the Kennet and Avon Canal.

The toll house was built before 1773. On the closure of the turnpike it was sold to Messrs. Hoare and Nicholl as trustees for the Marquis of Ailesbury.
VCH(xvi) WRO A1/205/11

Burbage (Southgrove)

Swindon, Marlborough and Everleigh Road 1761-1875

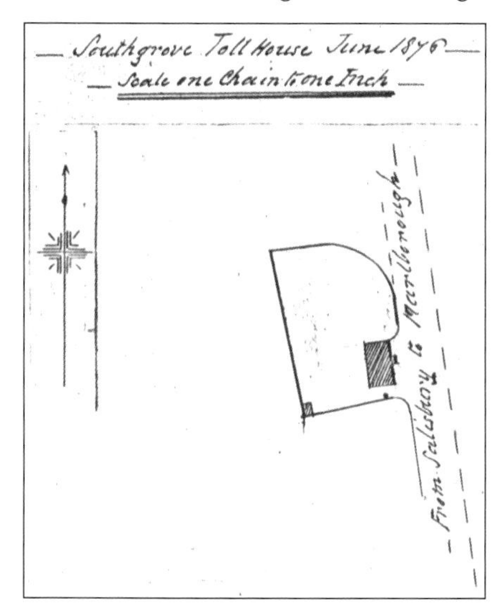

SU 225 591 On the A338 Marlborough to Salisbury road two miles south of Burbage near the entrance to Southgrove Copse.

The toll house was built between 1793 and 1817. On the closure of the turnpike it was sold to Messrs. Hoare and Nicholl as trustees of the Marquis of Ailesbury. The toll house (then known as Amsterdam Cottage) was still standing until at least 1998 and, after that, it was demolished and replaced by a new house.
VCH(xvi) WRO A1/205/11

Calne (Mile Elm)

Calne Roads/Calne and Devizes Roads 1706-1870

The original gate was at Smellings Lane. A toll house was established there in 1790 but was not purpose-built as the Trustees took over the lease of a house owned by the Marquis of Lansdowne 'in Smellings Lane on the New Road at or near Cold Harbour'. In 1792 a well was dug there for the use of the collector of tolls.

In 1859 the Trust decided to move the gate to Mile Elm. Again they did not build a new toll house but bought two existing cottages and converted them into a toll house. On the closure of the turnpike in 1871, the toll house and the adjoining cottage with their gardens were sold to Lord Lansdowne for £220. The property was described as being bounded on one side by the turnpike road leading from Calne to Melksham, on another side by garden ground belonging to Mr. Robert Henley and on all other sides by land and wood the property of the Marquis of Lansdowne.

TM(Calne) WRO A1/205/4

Calne (Quemerford)

Calne Roads/Calne and Devizes Roads 1706-1870

Little is known about this toll house. Certainly one existed there from an early date for, when William Skrine resigned as collector of tolls in 1803, the Trustees agreed to pay him seven shillings as compensation for the partition he had erected at his own expense in the kitchen of the toll house. There is also a reference in 1814 to a weighing engine previously erected at Quemerford Gate.

TM(Calne)

Calne Without (Chilvester Hill)

Calne Roads/Calne and Devizes Roads 1706-1870

A toll house certainly existed at Chilvester Hill by 1776 when John Aishley was appointed collector of tolls in place of William Perkins who had retired through age and infirmity. There is no further reference to the house until 1870 when the turnpike ended. The house was then sold to Lord Crewe for £80.

The plan and elevation (opposite) are probably c.1925 when the house was still in the possession of Lord Crewe. There had been at some stage a major extension and considerable internal alterations but the original toll house seems to have been of two storeys with two rooms on each floor.

TM(Calne) WRO 1794/11PC

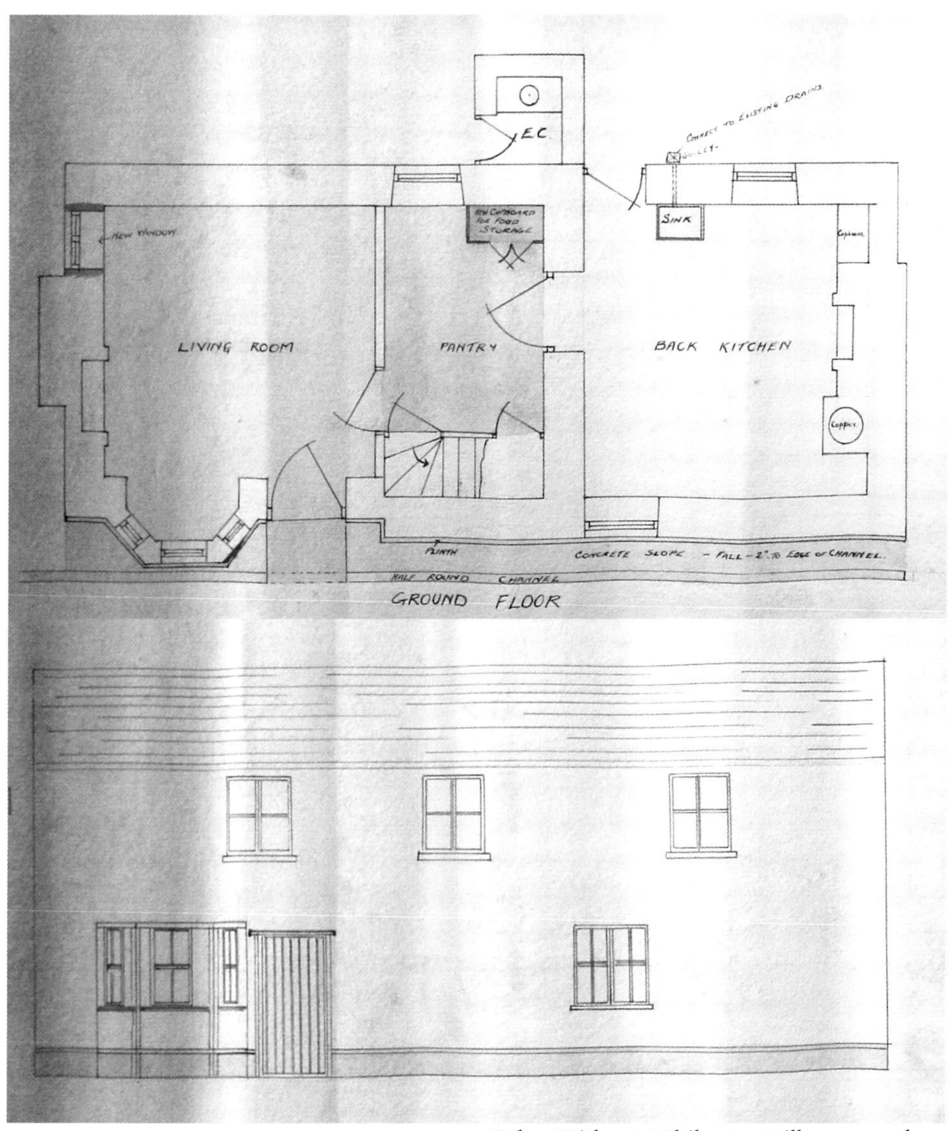

Calne Without (Chilvester Hill), c.1925 plans

Castle Combe (Salutation)
Sodbury and Cirencester Road 1751-1876

ST 838 791 On B4039 road from Castle Combe to Acton Turville where it crosses the Fosse Way

Very little is known about the toll house except for its sale towards the end of the turnpike's existence. It was bought by William Hulton of Hurst Grange, Lancaster, and his associates.
WRO A1/205/14

Charlton (Five Lanes)
Malmesbury Roads 1755-1874/6

ST 947 905 To the north of Malmesbury on the A429 road to Cirencester at Five Lanes.

Although various maps show a toll gate across the main road at the Five Lanes junction, the only evidence for the existence of a toll house there comes from the 1861 census. Sarah Townsend was then recorded as the toll collector living there with her husband, George, who was an agricultural labourer.

Charlton (The Street)
Malmesbury Roads 1755-1874/6

ST 962 889 On the B4040 Malmesbury to Cricklade Road

This toll house was probably built in the early 19th century. In the 1861 census the toll keeper at the Charlton Street gate was Hannah Wheeler, the wife of Edmund Wheeler who was an agricultural labourer.

There also seems to have been a toll house at the Perry Green gate to the east of Charlton. In 1861 the toll collector was Ann Honey whose husband, William, was also a labourer.

Chilmark (Chilmark)
Wilton Roads 1760-1870

SU 965 331 On the B3089 road from Wilton to Mere road to the west of Chilmark.

The evidence for the toll house comes from the closure of the turnpike in 1870 when the Trust sold the site to the Earl of Pembroke. It was then said that the Chilmark toll house had for many years stood on the site but had been or was about to be pulled down. The site was described as being bounded on the south by the turnpike road for 206 feet and on the west and north by land belonging to the Earl of Pembroke and in the occupation of William Bassett. There was also a strip of land held with the toll house on the other side of the road immediately opposite the toll house. The 1926 Ordnance Survey map shows a well on what had been the site of the toll house.
WRO A1/205/8

Chippenham (Bath Road)
Chippenham Roads 1726-1870

ST 909 725 At the junction of the A4 with the old Melksham road.

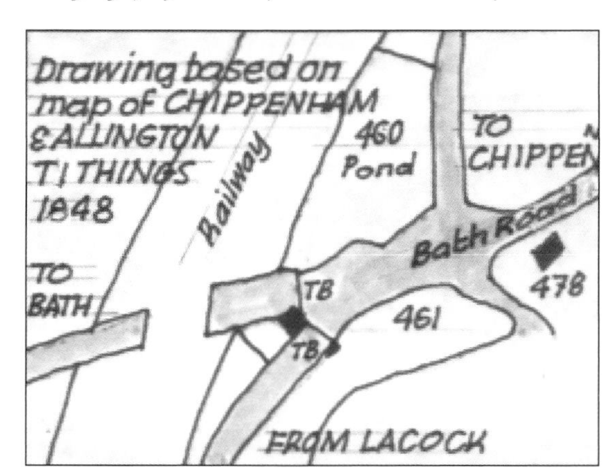

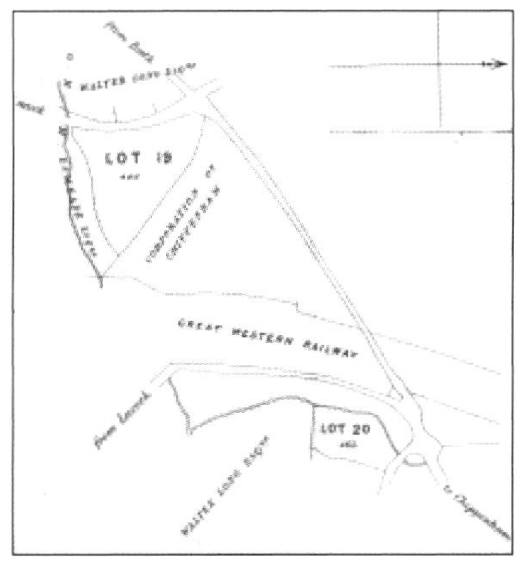

In 1834 the Trust undertook a major reorganisation of its toll gates in Chippenham. As part of this, the West gate was moved to the junction of the Lacock road with the Chippenham turnpike road. A tender for the erection of a new toll house associated with the gate was accepted from John Woodman of Chippenham, mason. The 1848 map shows the toll house in the fork of the roads to Bath and Melksham. The sale particulars in 1858 of a meadow 'near the Bath Road turnpike' also show a house in this position. In 1851 the house was occupied by Thomas Hornsey, aged 61, who was described as a Chelsea pensioner and toll taker. In the 1861 census the toll collector was Edward James, aged 68, who lived there with his wife, Lucy. On the closure of the turnpike in

1870, the house with its garden was sold by public auction. The photograph of the toll house intact is probably from the 1920s when it was occupied by Albert and Annie Deacon, who appear in the picture. The building was badly damaged by a lorry in August 1965, as depicted in the second photograph, and it was subsequently demolished.

TM(Chippenham) WRO 1769/97

Chippenham (Bridge)
Chippenham Roads 1726-1870

ST 920 734 At the east end of the bridge over the River Avon at the west end of the town.

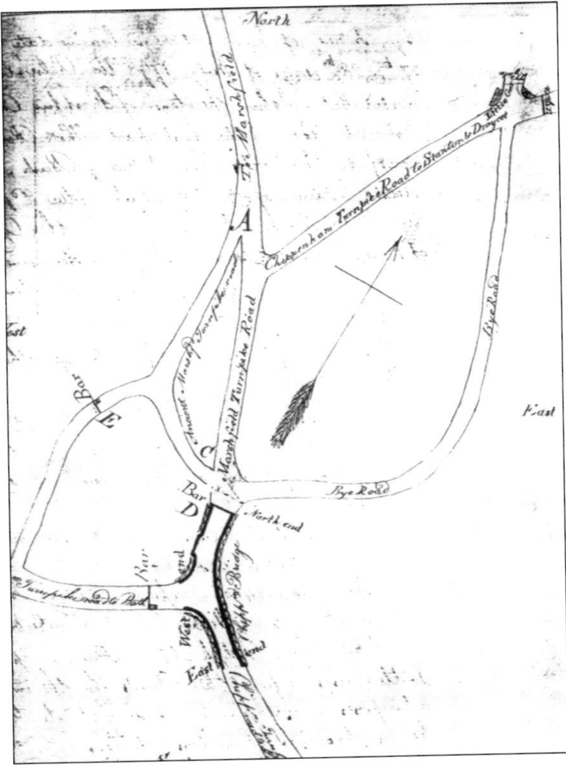

The arrangement of toll gates at the Bridge was complicated both because of the number of roads involved and also the connection with the Marshfield turnpike. Toll gates or bars were erected at the east, west and north ends of the bridge. A few years later, however, in agreement with the Marshfield Trust, a new bar was erected to the west (E on the above map). The bar at the north end of the bridge then became disused although a board with a list of toll charges remained on the wall of a house opposite. This was challenged in 1829 by Mr. Mason, the new lessee of the tolls, who tried to reintroduce charges at the north end of the bridge. The matter went to the High Court and Mr. Mason lost.

A toll house was probably built on the bridge soon after 1805. A minute of the Trust, which refers to the erection of the toll gates at the bridge, records the decision that 'toll houses be erected or provided for the collectors of the said tolls at or near the places where such gates or bars are to be erected.' Improvements were made to the house in 1826.

The substantial house in the above print has always been referred to as the Turnpike house or Higgins' house as if this was the same building. However, in October 1835 the Trust offered the Town Commissioners to take down and remove the old toll house near the bridge and, in its place, erect a new toll house on the Bath Road at the entrance to Hungerdown Lane near the cottages lately built by John Provis. The smaller, single storey house to the left of Higgins' house was more likely to be the toll house. It has disappeared in later pictures. Further confirmation comes from the censuses of 1851 and 1861 when Mr. Higgins, brazier and later ironmonger, is recorded as living at the bridge but there is no mention of a toll collector although the turnpike continued to operate until 1870.

TM(Chippenham) WRO 1780/34

Chippenham (Causeway)

Chippenham Roads 1726-1870

ST 924 729 At the Causeway on the A4 London Road.

The old photograph shows a typical two-storey toll house with a three-sided bay projecting towards the road.

Chippenham (Hungerdown Lane)
Chippenham Roads 1726-1870

ST 905 723 At the southern end of Hungerdown Lane at the old junction of the A4 and A350 opposite the Pheasant Inn (previously the New Inn).

In 1839 the Trust ordered a gate and toll house to be erected at or near a house in the occupation of Jonathan Webb called or known by the sign of the New Inn. The toll house is shown on the 1848 map and the 1851 census records the toll collector at the New Inn toll bar as Anne Church whose husband, Isaac, was a farm labourer. In 1861 William Robins was the toll collector and he was still there in 1871 after the turnpike had closed.
TM(Chippenham)

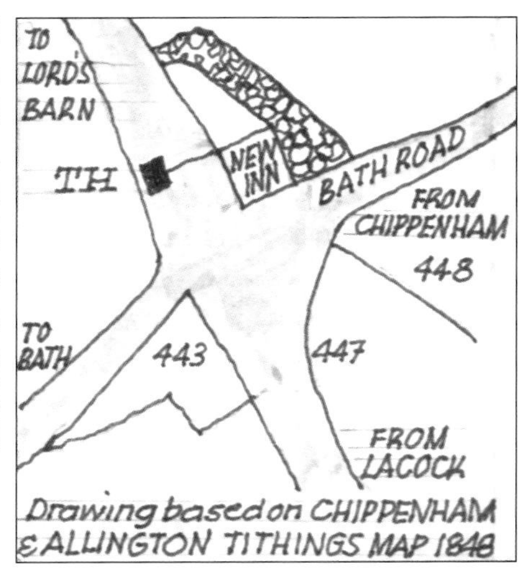

Chippenham (Little George)
Chippenham Roads 1726-1870

ST 919 739 At the junction of Malmesbury Road and Langley Road by St. Paul's church.

The toll house was probably built in 1822 when the Trust decided to erect a new gate at 'the entrance of Collett's Lane near Little George.' The map of 1829 (see *Chippenham (Bridge)*) shows a house in the fork of the two roads. The gate was removed in 1854 and, shortly afterwards, it was ordered that the toll house at Little George should be pulled down and the boundary wall of the churchyard made good.
TM(Chippenham)

Chippenham (London Road)
Chippenham Roads 1726-1870

ST 936 724 On the A4 Chippenham to Calne road at the junction with the unclassified road to Stanley.

As part of the major alteration of the Chippenham gates in 1834 the Trust decided to move the East gate to a site at or near Stanley Lane and the Surveyor was directed to find the best site to erect a toll house to serve the gate. In 1835 the Trust accepted a tender of £141 from John Woodman of Chippenham, mason, to erect the new toll house. It is a single storey brick house with a facetted stone façade to the main road. The central doorway, which is now blocked, is flanked by windows in the facets. It has a slate roof with a chimney stack at the apex. There is a two storey brick built house to the rear which appears to be contemporary.
TM(Chippenham)

Chippenham (Lowden)
London Roads 1726-1870

ST 915 733 On Lowden Hill just before the railway line.

In 1835 the Trust ordered that a new gate and toll house be erected at Lowden Lane. The site of the toll bar and house are shown on the 1848 map. The Chippenham Museum has a drawing by Jolliffe in 1866 which shows a relatively plain two-storey house. The photograph of the house as it now stands suggests that

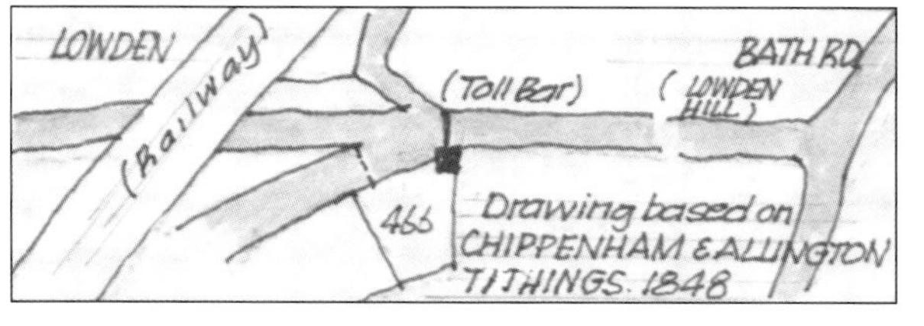

the left wing was the original toll house and the major extension added at a later date but probably not later than 1900.
TM(Chippenham)

Chippenham Without (Folly Gate)
Chippenham Roads 1726-1870

ST 905 742 At the south end of Hardenhuish Lane at the junction with the A420 Chippenham to Bristol road.

Listed Grade II 5/226

This two-storey house was probably built about 1830. It is of ashlar and coursed rubble stone under a slate roof. It has a three-sided canted bay with hipped roof on to the Bristol Road. On the east side is a gabled porch with slate roof. The house has been much extended in recent years.
LB

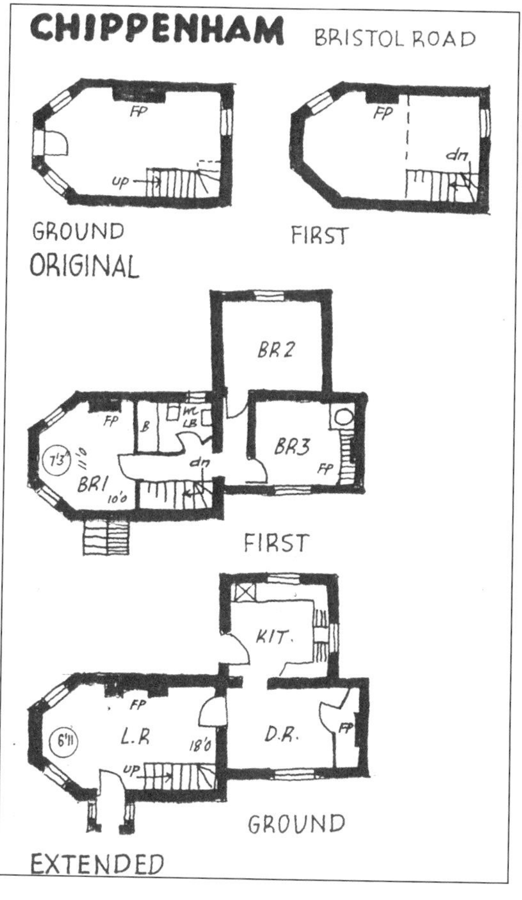

Chiseldon (Burderop)
Swindon, Marlborough and Everleigh Road 1761-1875

SU 163 799 On the B4005 Wroughton to Chiseldon road at the junction with the old turnpike road west of Burderop Farm.

Listed Grade II 15/30

This cottage looks to have been built in the mid 19th century. It is of two storeys, stucco with a hipped slate roof. The front to the road is angled with a window on each side and a central door, now blocked. Above the door is a 'blind' window.
LB

Chiseldon (Turnball)
Swindon and Hungerford Road 1815-1874

SU 184 796 On the B4005 in the middle of Chiseldon at the corner of Turnball and Hodson Road.

Listed Grade II 29/192

The original terrace of stone cottages under a thatched roof is late 17th century. A further cottage seems to have been added to this perhaps in the 18th century. Finally the red brick section, angled to Hodson Road, was added in the early 19th century to form the toll house. The turnpike room has a flagstone floor and low ceiling. To the north is a single storey thatched outbuilding.
LB

Clarendon Park (Petersfinger)
Salisbury and Southampton Roads 1753-1871

SU 164 292 On the A36 Salisbury to Southampton road at Petersfinger.

The minutes of the Trust record that in the first year of operation it decided to build three toll houses at Petersfinger, St. Thomas' Bridge and Eling. The cost of each toll house was not to exceed £30. Little more is known of the toll house until the closure of the Trust when the Petersfinger toll house was advertised for

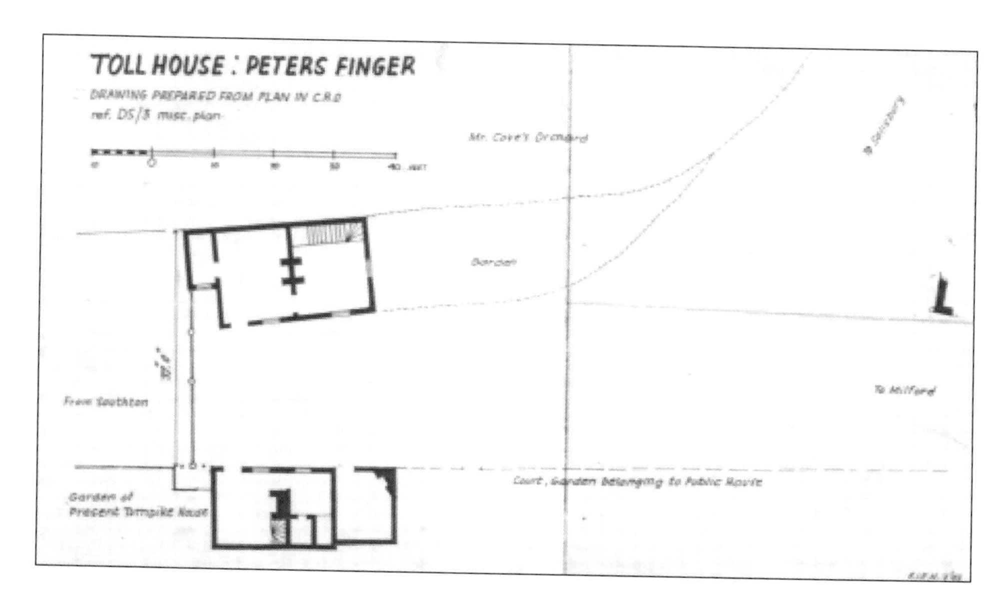

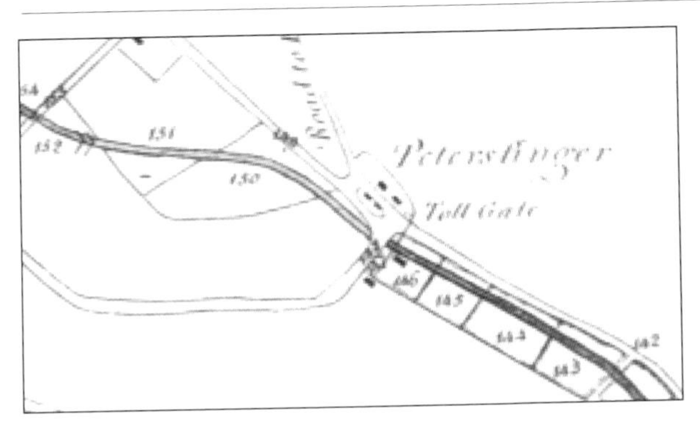

sale in the *Salisbury Journal.* It was then described as being brick built and tiled with a sitting room and kitchen, two bedrooms and a good wash-house.
TM(Sarum and Eling) SJ (3Apr70)

Collingbourne Ducis (Collingbourne Ducis)
Swindon, Marlborough and Everleigh Road 1761-1875

SU 244 536 On the A346 Ludgershall to Collingbourne Ducis road.

The only apparent evidence is the 1817 Ordnance Survey drawing which clearly shows a toll house at the junction of the roads from Ludgershall and Tidworth.

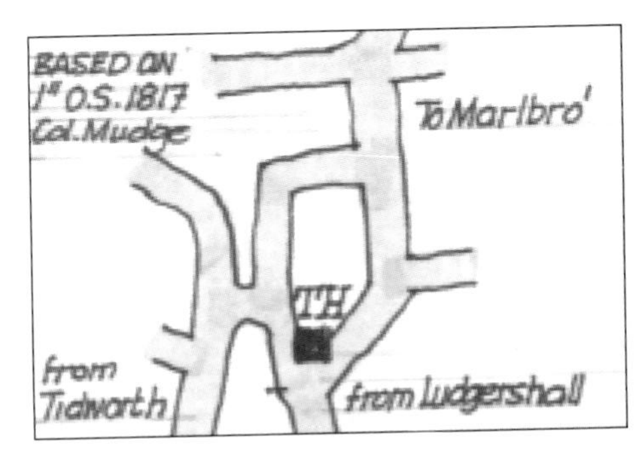

Corsley (Whitbourne)
Frome Roads 1757-1870

ST 839 442 On A362 Warminster to Frome Road at Whitbourne.

The toll house is situated on the Warminster to Frome road below Cley Hill. It has been considerably extended in recent times but the original projecting wing to the road is well preserved.
Houghton (Warminster)

Cricklade (The Dance)
Malmesbury Roads 1755-1874/6

SU 099 933 On the B4041 towards Purton near Dance Common.

The toll house was a relatively modest one standing on the road leading towards Purton but also controlling a side gate. A deed dated about 1850 refers to a messuage or tenement lately purchased by William Golding from Digby Coles. It was described as at Cricklade on the Cricklade and Wootton Bassett turnpike road at or near the junction with Vorty (now Forty) Lane, part of which messuage was the Vorty side gate toll house. The house was demolished in 1964.
WRO 700/134/3

Cricklade (Malmesbury Road)
Malmesbury Roads 1755-1874/6

SU 095 936 In Cricklade on the Bath Road at Culverhay Cross.

This was a very simple toll house reminiscent of that at Amesbury (Countess Road). It was of stone with a stone roof and exterior chimney stack on the east elevation. There was probably a simple porch over the door leading on to the road and a toll board under the ground floor window. The house was knocked down in 1968.

Crudwell (Crudwell)

Malmesbury Roads 1755-1874/6

ST 952 927 On A429 Malmesbury to Cirencester road at Crudwell just north of the road leading to North Newnton.

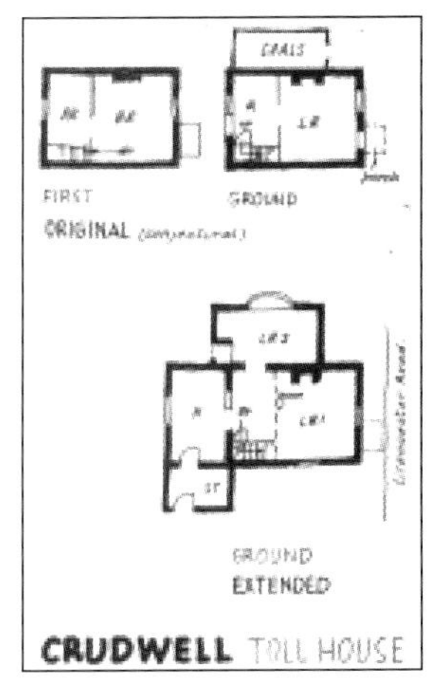

The Toll House. The original house was of stone with two storeys but very modest with probably only two rooms on each floor. It was later extended at right angles. Unfortunately no further documentary evidence has been found to expand on the history of the house.

Crudwell (Eastcourt)
Cirencester and Wootton Bassett Road 1810-1863

ST 977 927 At the north east of the crossing of the unclassified roads Hankerton-Oaksey and Minety-Crudwell.

The road was turnpiked in 1810 and what had been a staggered cross roads was re-aligned and a toll house built to the north east. The Trust accounts for 1810 record 'To amount expended in making the said Branch Road and for the erecting of a Turnpike House and gates at Eastcourt and Minety £1200'. On the closure of the turnpike in 1863 a dispute arose over the ownership of the house. The clerk, Mr. Ellett, wrote to Richard Cummings of Eastcourt House offering to sell the house to the estate: 'The Eastcourt Toll house seems to be a better house than the others and to be a desirable one for the owner of Eastcourt to possess in its present state. The Trustees hope Mrs. Mullings will be willing to take this house at £100.' Richard Cummings consulted a previous surveyor of the turnpike and he wrote to say that in 1841 everyone understood that the Trust had not built the toll house and that it belonged to Joseph Mullings. He also reminded them that at least from 1842 to 1845 the Trust was paying an annual rent of £3 10s. for the toll house to the Eastcourt Estate. Even so Ellett still maintained that his records clearly showed the house was owned by the Trust. It is not clear how the dispute was resolved but when the Eastcourt Estate was sold in 1883, the sale included a cottage and garden on the site of the toll house. The house was demolished some years ago.
WRO 374/58 WRO 374/130/35 VCH(xiv)

Devizes (Besborough)
Devizes Roads 1706-1868

SU 001 617 In Northgate Street at the point where it crosses the canal.

The old London to Bristol road originally ran along the line of the present canal and was diverted to its present position when the canal was built.

Besborough Lodge is a substantial, stone built, two-storey house with its hexagonal end facing the main road. After the realignment of the road, it became the canal lock keeper's cottage.

Devizes (The Green)
Devizes Roads 1706-1868

SU 011 615 On the A361 road from Beckhampton by the Green to the north of St. James's church.

Although not large, the toll house was an impressive building with a classical portico. It commanded an important position alongside St. James's Church at the eastern entrance to Devizes. When the Trust closed in 1868 the toll house with its adjacent outbuildings, small garden, well and pump was valued at £75. It was offered to Mr. John Perry, the owner of the adjoining land, but he would give only £50 for it because the roof and windows needed repair. The Trust declined this bid and, instead, ordered the toll house to be pulled down and its materials sold.

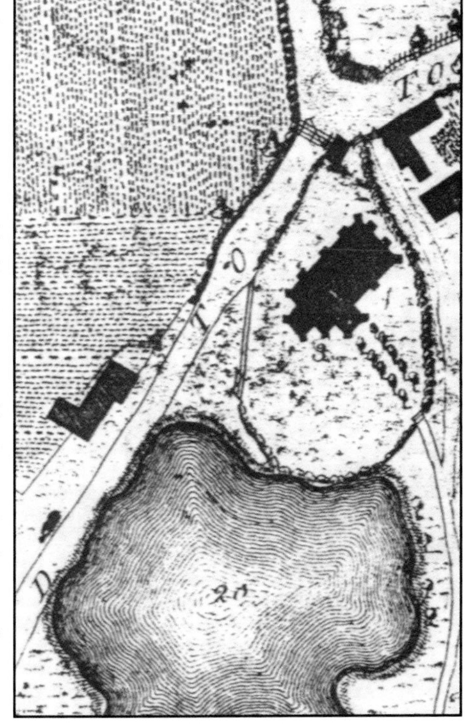

TM(Devizes), Dore's town map, 1759

Devizes (Shane's Castle)
Devizes Roads 1706-1868

ST 996 617 At the junction of the A342 (Devizes – Chippenham) and A365 (Devizes – Melksham/Trowbridge).

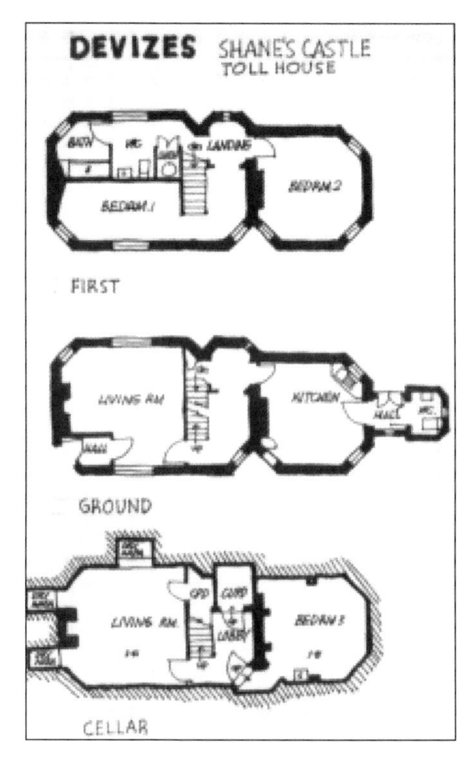

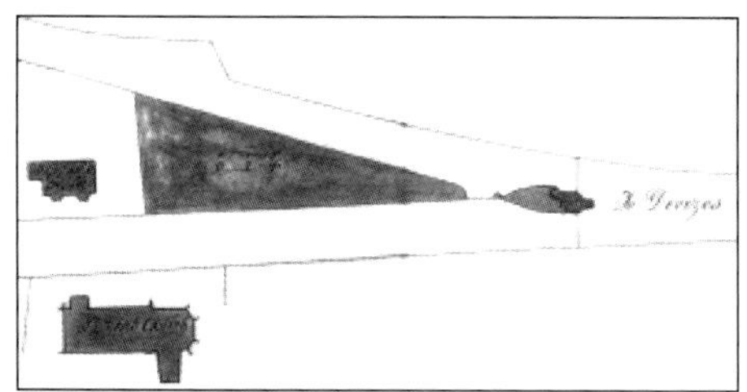

Listed Grade II 1/186

The house was built in the early 19th century. The small, two-storey building is very distinctive consisting in plan of an octagon joined to a rectangle of the same width. It has a small, square one-storey porch on the east end. The building is distinguished by its battlement cresting. There is strong evidence to suggest that the rectangular section to the west was added at a later date.

On the closure of the turnpike in 1868, the toll house and adjoining land was sold for £185 to the county through William Merriman, Clerk of the Peace. The land to the west of the toll house was already owned by the county and was used by the Royal Wiltshire Militia as their depot. The deed identifies the small garden attached to the toll house and enclosed with iron fencing. Also there was the larger piece of land, containing 40 poles, which extended to the house occupied by Captain Belliers, the adjutant of the Royal Wiltshire Militia.
LB TM(Devizes) WRO A1/205/7

Devizes (Wick Green)
Devizes Roads 1706-1868

SU 005 605 On A360 Devizes to Salisbury road at the junction with Wick Lane.

This was a relatively modest brick built toll house with a stone roof. The gable ends and porch originally had decorative 'gothic' bargeboards. When the Trust

closed in 1868 the tollhouse was sold to the Estcourt estate for £50. At some later date the toll house was demolished to improve the visibility at the junction of Wick Lane.
WRO A1/205/7

Dilton Marsh (Clivey)
Westbury Roads 1757-1872

ST 838 501 On B3099 Westbury to Beckington road on the western outskirts of Dilton Marsh.

Listed Grade II 3/104

This two-storey cottage was probably built in the mid

19th century and has substantial additions of the 20th century. It is of rendered brick and has a tile roof with fishscale bands. There is a two-storey canted front facing the road with a central doorway which is now blocked. The two sides have blind lozenges and blocked pointed doorways.
LB

East Knoyle (East Knoyle)
Shaftesbury and Sherborne Roads 1753-1877

ST 881 306 On the A350 Warminster to Shaftesbury road.

The evidence for this toll house comes from the 1861 census. The toll collector living there was William Hunt with his wife, Elizabeth, and their grandson, Charles. The settlement beyond the southern end of the East Knoyle by-pass is still known as 'Turnpike' and one house there is named Turnpike Cottage.

Edington (Ivy Mill)
Seend to Trowbridge and Beckington Road 1751-1870

ST 925 542 Turnpike Cottage. One mile south of Edington at Ivy Mill on the unclassified road to Steeple Ashton.

The original red brick house had round arched windows and an external stack on the side towards Edington. It ran back from the road and is said to have been 'one up and one down.' A brick extension was added on the north side in the late 19th or early 20th century with a further extension on the same side in the late 20th century. It is now a farm cottage for Ivy Mill Farm (illustrated overleaf).

Edington (Ivy Mill)

Froxfield (Harrow Farm)
London to Bath Road 1725-1871

SU 275 679 On the A4 Marlborough to Hungerford road at the cross roads by Harrow Farm.

Little is known about this toll house. It was in existence in 1846 and a deed records its sale to the Marquis of Ailesbury in 1871. It appears to have been demolished in the late 19th century.
WRO A1/205/10 VCH(xvi)

Great Hinton (Cold Harbour)
Seend to Trowbridge and Beckington Road 1751-1870

ST 901 588 On the unclassified Keevil to Trowbridge road at Cold Harbour.

The only reference is in a deed of 1906 which refers to 'two messuages and tenements or dwelling houses with the subbuildings and gardens situate at Cold Harbour formerly in the tything of Hinton in the parish of Steeple Ashton and now in the parish of Hinton and adjoining the late turnpike road there and containing 20 perches part whereof was formerly used as a toll house formerly in the occupation of William Cooper'.
WRO 816/182

Grittleton (Jockey)

Pucklechurch and Christian Malford Road 1755-1873

ST 873 805 On the unclassified road from Grittleton to Stanton St Quintin about two miles to the east of Grittleton.

The original gate seems to have been situated near Clapcote Quarry. At some time it was moved to a site near Jockey Cottages to the east of Grittleton and a nearby cottage was leased from John Neeld for a toll house. In 1850 John Neeld asked for re-possession of the cottage and this was agreed by the Trustees. The intention then was to move the gate back to its original site near Clapcote Quarry and to build a new toll house there. But when the tenders had been received, the Trustees changed their minds and, instead, ordered that the gate be kept at Jockey with only a toll box. This was to be wooden with an iron stove and 'to be built at the least expense'. A year later the Trustees agreed to some improvement to the toll house at a cost not exceeding £5.

On the closure of the turnpike, the 'toll house and site including the turnpike gate' was sold to Sir John Neeld for £5. The small amount involved seems to confirm that the 'toll house' was indeed simply the wooden box and its site.
TM(Christian Malford)

Heddington (Heddington)

Old London to Bath Road 1713-1790

ST 981 663 On the unclassified road from Heddington to Sandy Lane just west of Heddington Wick.

The old London to Bath road ran past Heddington then across Beacon Hill towards Avebury. As traffic began to use the Bristol road through Calne, the old road became less used and was disturnpiked in 1790. The house was probably built in 1713 making it one of the earliest toll houses. It is of red brick with stone dressings and mullioned windows with hood moulds. The gable end with a central door faces the road. It was enlarged at a later

date with wings at right angles to the original house. It is now known as Turnpike Farm.
VCH (xvii)

Highworth (Westrop)
Burford to Lechlade Road 1792-1875

SU 202 928 On the main road from Highworth to Lechlade.

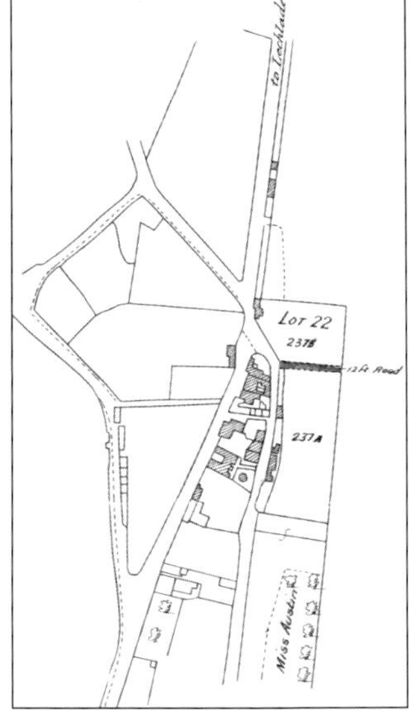

The toll house was a very modest, single storey building probably with only two rooms. In the photograph (above) the right hand section was a later addition and the original doorway blocked up. The house was demolished in about 1975. Its site is now rather lost in the pattern of new roads and housing estates in the north of Highworth When the turnpike was closed, the house was sold in 1876 for £30 to Rev. Eyre Hussey of Lyneham and George Eyre of Bramshaw. It was sold out of the Hussey Freke estates in 1908 for £72 10s. Its position was then described as 'being bounded on the west by the main road leading from Highworth to Lechlade, on the south-west by a road leading

off the main road to the back part of Highworth and on all other sides by land owned by the vendors (i.e. Hussey-Freke)'.
WRO 776/468 WRO G6/150/1

Hilmarton (Snow Hill)

Swindon, Calne and Cricklade Roads 1790-1879

In 1793 the Trust erected a gate across the road at Snow Hill at a house occupied by William Chivers, a labourer. They then appointed William Chivers and his wife, Sarah, as collectors of the tolls at a salary of 3s. 6d. a week.
TM(Swindon, Calne, Cricklade)

Hilperton (Devizes Road)

Trowbridge Roads 1751-1870

ST 873 590 On the A361 at the junction with the B3105 opposite the Lion and Fiddle.

The earlier pictures show this as a single storey building with a central door and porch flanked by windows in blind arches. When the turnpike was closed in 1870 the house and yard was sold for £83 to George Dunsdon of Hilperton, a labourer.

At some later stage the house was raised to two storeys but the basic plan remained unchanged.

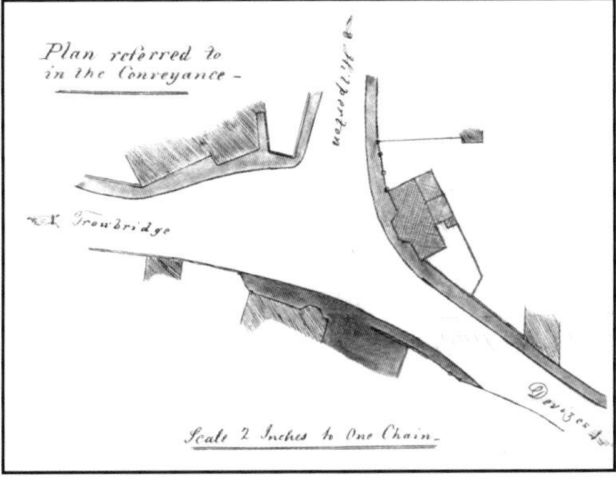

The projecting porch was also raised and a roof similar to that on the original building was retained. The roof is now tiled.
WRO A1/205/18

Hilperton (Hilperton)
Trowbridge Roads 1751-1870

ST 872 593 On the B3105 in the centre of Hilperton.

This two-storey stone built house has a door in the curved projecting single storey wing on the south end of the house. It has tall, narrow circular headed ground floor windows and a tiled roof. Doubts have been raised whether this was a toll house because of its position at the junction with a very minor lane. But there is now positive evidence to remove this doubt.

In 1869 there was a petition (successful) to a House of Commons committee to discontinue the Trust. The main argument against the Trustees was that they had been extravagant in their expenditure, especially on toll houses, and had neglected to redeem their debts. One toll house in particular was picked out for criticism as 'a residence with bedrooms, with a toll house, in a side lane between two other toll houses'. Later correspondence refers to this toll house as being at a side lane near Hilperton Gate.

When the turnpike closed in 1870 the Trust sold a piece of land (3¾ perches) with a toll house (called Middle Lane toll house) to Richard Long of Rood Ashton.

The land was described as being part of plot 118 on the tithe map i.e. the site of the present house. The tithe map is dated 1838 but does not contain the toll house which must have been built about 1840-50 along with other new toll houses by the Trowbridge Trust.
WRO A1/205/18 TNW Ad (8May69, 22May69)

Holt (Holt)
Holt Roads 1761-1873

ST 857 616 On the B3107 Bradford-on-Avon to Melksham road on the western edge of the village at the junction with the road to Staverton.

The toll gate at Holt was on the western edge of the village by the Common and is commemorated by the Tollgate public house. The old picture of about 1875 (overleaf, top) clearly shows the gate although the actual toll house is less clear. It may be the end house of the existing terrace of cottages. The drawing (by Jack Thierens in *The Story of Holt, 3*), based on a photograph, seems to show the end cottage with a board of charges and lamp, and the gates further north. A modern photo of the end cottage of Ham Terrace is at the foot of the page overleaf.

Idmiston (Gomeldon)

Swindon, Marlborough and Everleigh Road 1761-1875

SU 181 360 On the A338 Salisbury to Marlborough road at Gomeldon.

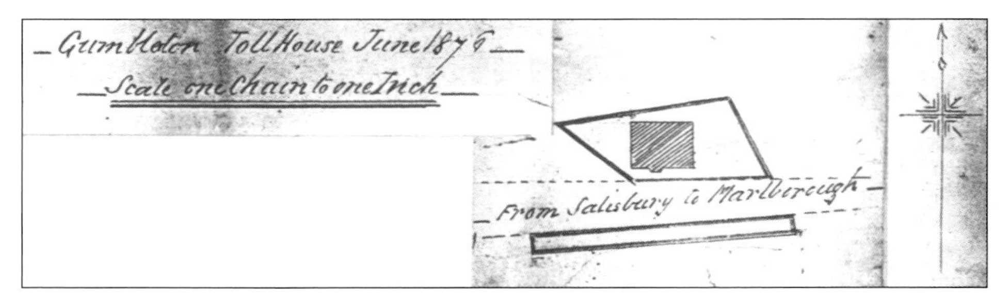

The evidence for the existence of a toll house at Gomeldon comes from its sale in 1876 for £67 to Joseph Waters, gentleman, of Gomeldon. The house was then described as being on the northern side of the turnpike road and bounded on all other sides by lands of Joseph Waters. The sale included a garden of 3½ perches on the southern side of the road and immediately opposite the toll house.
WRO A1/205/11

Keevil (The Strand)

Trowbridge Roads 1751-1870

ST 924 596 On the A361 Trowbridge to Devizes road at the corner of Keevil Lane.

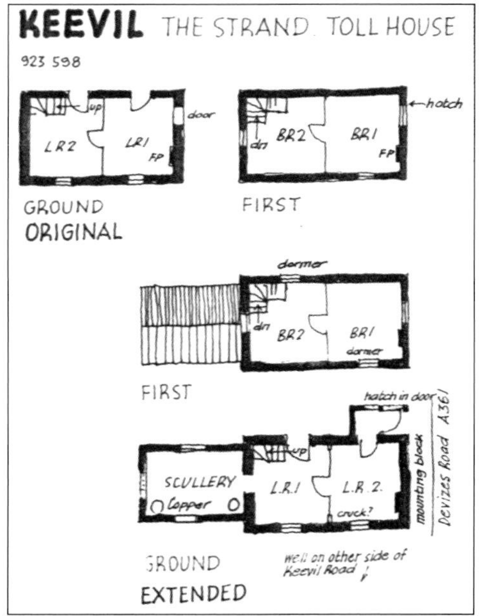

This was a very modest 18th century stone toll house with a stone tiled roof. It originally had two rooms on the ground floor and two above, the scullery to the east being added at a later date. The rooms were inter-communicating and divided by boarded partitions. A narrow, winding and boxed stair was located in one corner. On the north side there was a hatch for collecting tolls. Water was available from a well on the other side of the road to Keevil. When the Trust closed in 1870, the house was sold for £50 to George Bartlett of

Edmonton, Middlesex. The house continued to be occupied well into the 1950s but in recent years it was unoccupied and gradually became derelict as it was robbed for its building materials. Only the walls to eaves level remain.
WRO A1/205/18

Kingston Deverill (Pertwood)
Warminster Roads 1726-1870

SU 882 353 On the A350 at the crossroads East Knoyle to Warminster and Hindon to Monkton Deverill.

The only information on this toll house comes from the sale particulars of the property of the Trust when it closed in 1870. It was then sold to the Marquis of Bath who already owned the land next to the toll house.
WRO A1/205/19

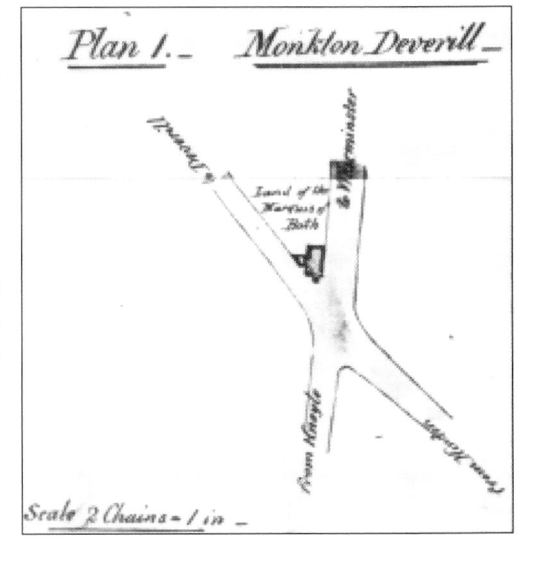

Langley Burrell Without (Langley Common)

Chippenham Roads 1726-1870

ST 925 749 On the A420 road towards Sutton Benger at the junction with Hill Corner Road (previously Greenway Lane) at Langley Common.

When the Trust closed the gate at Little George, Chippenham in 1854 they decided to replace it with a new gate at the corner of Greenway Lane at Langley Common. The Clerk was instructed to communicate with the owners of the land on either side of Greenway Lane with a view to procuring sufficient land to erect a toll house. They settled on a site abutting a field in the occupation of John Knight, junior. But almost immediately afterwards the Rev. Ashe of Langley Burrell offered to give the Trust an alternative, nearby piece of land which seems to have been part of the field occupied by John Knight. The Trust accepted the offer and erected a toll house there. In the 1861 census the collector of tolls at the Langley Common turnpike was Samuel James.
TM(Chippenham)

Laverstock (Old Sarum)

Salisbury and Southampton Roads 1753-1870

SU 141 326 On the A345 at the junction of the Salisbury-Amesbury road with the old road to Marlborough.

This is a two-storey red brick house with a slate-hung front end and side elevations bonded with flints. Each side elevation has two triangular headed gothic windows. A later porch obscures the original doorway.

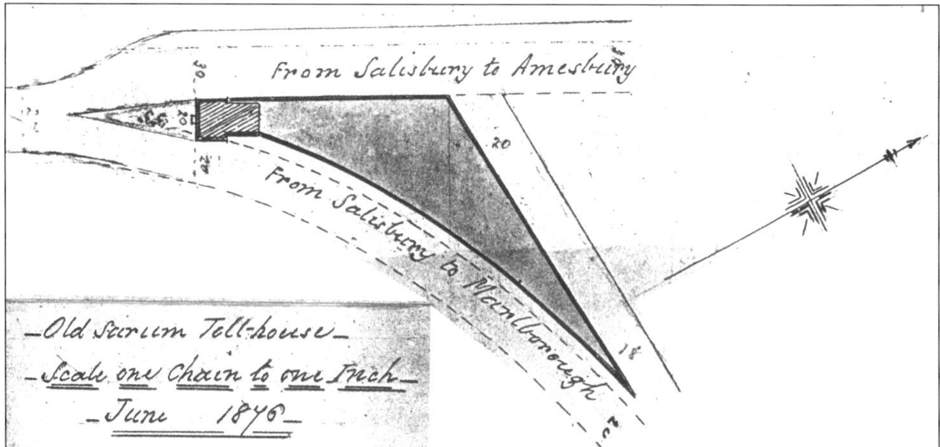

On the closure of the turnpike in 1876, the house was sold by the Trustees to the Salisbury Dean and Chapter through their clerk, Fitzherbert Macdonald, for £100. It was then described as 'a messuage or tenement lately used as a toll house and called the Old Sarum Toll House with the garden and appurtenances.' Subsequently it was let to Robert Marchment of Stratford-sub-Castle at a rent of 2s. 6d. a week. Locally always referred to as 'The Beehive', and recently restored, it has given its nickname to the modern Park and Ride facility nearby.
WRO A1/205/11 WRO CC/Chap 24C/1,2

Laverstock (St. Thomas's Bridge)
Salisbury and Southampton Roads 1753-1870

SU 165 321 Situated to the north of Salisbury near St. Thomas's bridge at the junction of the A338 and A30.

The original house at the toll gate was built in 1753. At the bar there was also a smaller building described as a 'wooden house'. This seems to have been replaced in 1841 by a more permanent building. In 1857 it was reported that the toll house (probably the one at the bar) was unoccupied and there was concern that 'if this is allowed, the place will certainly become dilapidated and mischievous parties will no doubt break the windows and cause other damage'. It was agreed therefore that the man at the gate should be given the opportunity of placing a tenant in the house for so long a period as the Trustees thought proper.
TM(Salisbury and Eling)

Liddington (Liddington)
Swindon and Hungerford Road 1813-1874

SU 206 815 7, The Street, in the centre of Liddington village.
The toll house is gable end on to the road at a fork in the centre of the village. It is now called Byways but was previously known as Turnpike Cottage. Village tradition also recalls it as being a toll house.
SP(Lidd)

Longbridge Deverill (Crockerton)
Warminster Roads 1726-1870

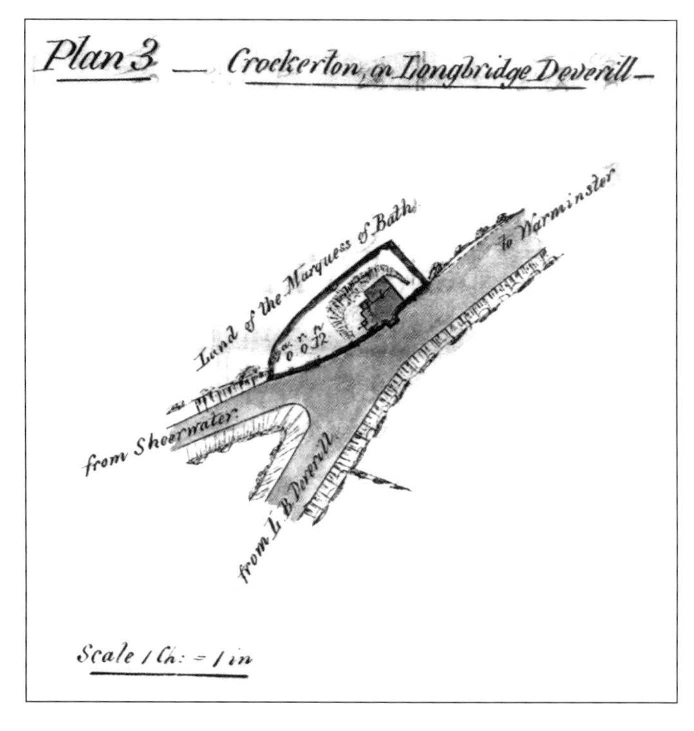

ST 864 427 On old A350 Warminster to East Knoyle road in Crockerton at junction with road leading to Shear Water.
The toll house was built in 1840 by George Edwards at a cost of £127. It has been extensively modernised in recent times. On the closure of the turnpike in 1870 the toll house was sold to the Marquis of Bath.
WRO A1/205/19
Houghton (Warminster)

Lyneham (Lyneham)
Swindon, Calne and Cricklade Roads 1790-1879

There appears to have been, at various times, three gates with associated toll houses in Lyneham but the position is complicated because the Trust moved two of them at least once. In 1792 a house occupied by Thomas Milsom near Hobb's House was taken over by the Trust and Milsom and his wife became collectors of the tolls. Also a gate was erected in Church End Lane near the house occupied by Jacob Eatwell, a blacksmith, who also became collector of the tolls. In 1794 the gates were re-sited although the resulting arrangement is not entirely clear. One gate appears to have been sited at the junction of Church End Lane and Preston Lane and a new toll house built there. Another gate was said to be in Hobb's Lane near the new house built by Mr. Heneage and which the Trust agreed to rent for two guineas a year. Finally, a map of the Methuen estate in 1830 shows a toll bar and house just outside Lyneham on the road to Wootton Bassett. A Lyneham toll board is displayed in Lyneham public library.
TM(Swindon,Calne,Cricklade) WRO 1742

Malmesbury St. Paul Without (Burton Hill)
Malmesbury Roads 1755-1874/6

ST 934 864 On the A429 Chippenham to Malmesbury road on the southern outskirts of Malmesbury.
Listed Grade II 5/143 Pike House, Burton Hill.

This single-storey house is early 19th century with late 20th century rear additions. It is of squared and coursed rubble with a front of squared and coursed dressed ashlar. There are two canted bays on brackets with triangular-headed sash windows under a single slate roof.
LB

Market Lavington (Black Dog)
Devizes Roads 1706-1868

ST 995 558 On the A360 Devizes to Salisbury road at the junction with the unclassified road to Worton.

It appears that a toll house was built or acquired here quite early but also disposed of after a relatively short time. A deed of 1783 records the sale by John Street to John Sainsbury for £16 of a house, lately used as a toll house, 'situate and lying at a place called Deweys ... on a certain spot at the end of a lane leading to Worton'. He said he had bought the house from the Market Lavington turnpike road in 1782. The Sainsbury family sold the house to Charles Money Kyrle for £20 in 1870. It was then described as being nearly opposite the Black Dog public house on the road from Devizes to Lavington.
WRO 402/124 WRO 542/42

Marlborough (Marlborough Common)
Swindon, Marlborough and Everleigh Road 1761-1875

SU 179 701 On Marlborough Common on the road to Rockley.

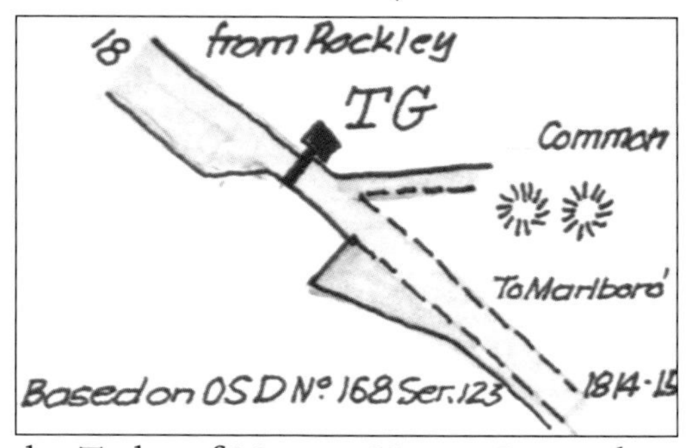

It is not certain when the toll house was built. A toll house was in existence in 1767 for a coroner's report records the sudden death of Henry Haggard while travelling along the road by the turnpike house on Marlborough Common. On the closure of the turnpike the toll house was sold for £70 to Alexander Taylor of Manton House. It was then described as being situated on the east side of the turnpike road and at the north west of Marlborough Common. It also had a garden containing 30 perches on the west side of the road opposite the toll house. At the time of the 1881 census the Newman family were gatekeepers.
WRO A1/205/17

Marlborough (St. Margaret's)
Swindon, Marlborough and Everleigh Road 1761-1875

SU 194 684 On the A 346 Marlborough to Salisbury road one mile south of Marlborough.

On the closure of the turnpike the toll house was sold to Messrs. Hoare and Nicholl as trustees of the Marquis of Ailesbury. It seems likely that the house became a lodge for the Savernake estate. The 1925 Ordnance Survey 6' map shows the site as Salisbury Road Lodge Gate but it is now known as Salisbury Hill Lodge. The present ornate lodge (listed grade II 2/302) has a date stone (1886) over the porch and the original toll house must have been either completely remodelled or demolished and re-built.

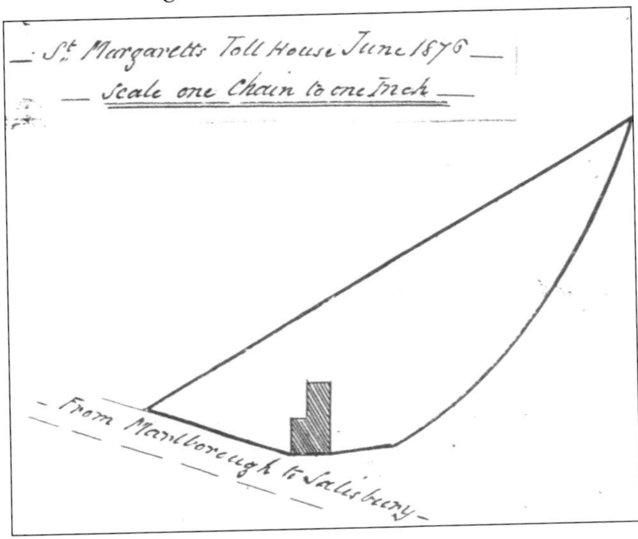

WRO A1/205/11

Melksham (Challeymead)
Melksham Roads 1753-1873

ST 903 642 At the junction of Old Broughton Road and New Broughton Road.

The 1773 map shows a gate on the road from Holt before it meets the old Bath Road. There is recollection of a toll house, now demolished, in the fork where the Old Broughton Road meets the New Broughton Road.

Melksham (Lowbourne)
Melksham Roads 1753-1873

There is an early reference in the Trust minutes to a toll house on the road leading from Melksham to the Forest but it is not clear how or whether this relates to Lowbourne. In 1767 the gate was moved further down the road to a

house belonging to John Prutty and occupied by Jacob Wilshire and his wife, Mary. They then became the toll collectors at a salary of 3s. 6d. a week. In Lowbourne the present Bulgin's (or Lowbourne) Villas are, according to their deeds, built on the site of an old toll house.
TM(Box, Seend)

Melksham (Melksham)
Melksham Roads 1753-1878

ST 905 635 In the centre of Melksham at the junction of the Market Place and Spa Road.

The stone toll house was quite substantial with a two-storey projecting bay. Its date is uncertain although the print is from about 1830.

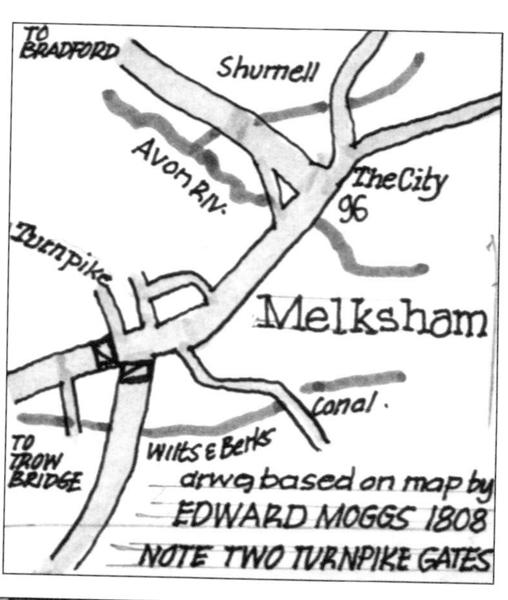

Melksham (Semington Lane)
Westbury Roads 1757-1872

ST 904 634 In King Street leading to Semington Road almost opposite Orchard Gardens.

This relatively simple toll house has its gable end to the road with a central door and stone porch. The house seems to have been extended to the rear at some time. It is said that the last turnpike keeper was Abram Bolland, an old soldier and veteran of the Indian Mutiny.
MHA(Melksham in Old Photos)

Melksham Without (Bowerhill)
Melksham Roads 1753-1878

ST 928 621 On A365 Melksham to Devizes road next to Turnpike Garage.

The toll house was a typically modest low building of three rooms including the projecting wing. It was extended to the west in 1975 and the projecting wing was re-built in the 1980s after a car had demolished that part of the

building. It is reported that inside the wing were the original drawers for keeping cash.

It is not certain when the toll house was built but it was probably in the 19th century rather than on the establishment of the turnpike trust in 1753. There could have been an earlier house in the vicinity used as the toll house. A Trust minute of 1783 records the decision to erect a chain or bar at a house owned by Robert Sims, a carpenter, opposite a lane leading to Crays Marsh across the road leading from Melksham to Seend. Robert Sims and his wife, Edith, then became the toll collectors.

The present house, on the closure of the turnpike in 1878, was sold for £105 to George Gingell, a general dealer from Redstocks.
TM(Box,Seend)

Mildenhall (Savernake)
London to Bath Road 1725-1871

SU 208 684 On the A4 Marlborough to Hungerford road a mile to the east of Marlborough.

It has been claimed that this 'Strawberry Hill Gothick' house was a lodge for the Savernake estate. It now seems clear, however, that it was a toll house as described in the details of the recent sale of Woodland House in whose grounds it now stands. It was almost certainly sold to the trustees of the Marquis of

Ailesbury on the closure of the turnpike. It was then described as being on Marlborough Hill in or near the edge of Savernake Forest and bounded in part by the turnpike road and on all other sides by land of the Marquis of Ailesbury. It had a stable and garden and also, behind it, a cottage and garden occupied by John Shipman.
WRO A1/205/10

Ogbourne St. Andrew (Rockley)
Swindon, Marlborough and Everleigh Road 1761-1875

The toll house was situated in Rockley but its exact position is unknown. On the closure of the turnpike it was sold in 1876 for £20 to Robert Tanner of Rockley House.
WRO A1/205/20

Ogbourne St. George (Southend)
Marlborough and Coate Road 1819-1874

SU 198 734 Situated on the A345 Swindon to Marlborough road at Ogbourne St. George opposite Hallam Road.

Listed Grade II 7/86

The toll house is on a cross roads in the centre of the village and a map of 1832 suggests there were gates across the main turnpike road and also across the side roads leading to Woodbury Hill and to Hallam. The original cottage is of the 17th century but it has been much altered in recent times. It is of flint with limestone dressings and timber-framed gables under a thatched roof. There is a 20th century slated brick lean-to at the rear. This seems to be an example of an existing cottage being taken over in the 19th century and adapted for use as a toll house.

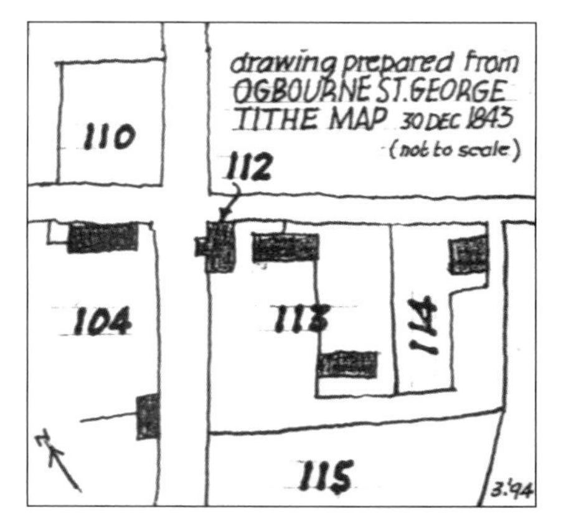

In the 1861 census the occupiers were William and Eliza Chunn. Eliza, aged 63, was listed as the toll collector while her husband was a brickmaker.
LB

Poulshot (Poulshot Lodge)
Devizes Roads 1706-1868

ST 974 613 On A361 Trowbridge to Devizes road at the junction with the unclassified road to Poulshot.

It is not certain when this toll house was built. In 1848 the Surveyor reported that the 'old' turnpike toll house was in a bad state of repair. He recommended

that the old stable on the opposite side of the road be pulled down and the materials used to repair the toll house. This did not seem to have happened for in 1868 the Trust sold the detached brick built stable and garden on the north side of the road for £33 to Mr. Weaver, an architect and surveyor. At the same time the toll house with walled-in garden and workshop was sold to Mr Long M.P. for £75.

This is probably the same house (see photo above) which was sold by auction in 1911. It was then described as being situated at the corner of the main road from Devizes to Trowbridge and Devizes to Poulshot. It consisted of a detached cottage, brick built and slated, containing four rooms, a large garden and a woodshed.

TM(Devizes) WRO A1/205/7

Preshute (Preshute)

Beckhampton Roads 1742-1870

There is very little evidence about this toll house and its location. In 1857 the Beckhampton Trust decided to erect a new toll gate with a toll house 'at the entrance to Marlborough at or near a place called the Quaker's burial ground.' It is assumed that this was at Preshute for the Trust then accepted a tender of £120 from C. E. Pinniger to build the Preshute toll house. When the turnpike ended in 1870, the Trust offered to sell the house to Lord Ailesbury but he declined it. The house was then pulled down and the materials sold.

WRO A1/205/11 TM(Beckhampton) WRS(xxxvi)

Purton (Collins Lane)

Swindon, Calne and Cricklade Roads 1790-1879

SU 095 891 On the B4041 Purton to Cricklade road, north of Purton at the Collins Lane and Station Road junction.

Listed Grade II 8/339
This early 19th century toll cottage is of limestone rubble, partly rendered and with a slate roof. The cottage is of two storeys on a hexagonal plan with a large later extension to the rear. The roof has a canted overhang to the front. The original front doorway is now blocked but, above it, remains the painted toll board with prescribed stages and charges.
LB

Roundway (Nursteed)
Devizes Roads 1706-1868

SU 021 601 On the A342 Devizes to Upavon road on the eastern outskirts of Devizes.

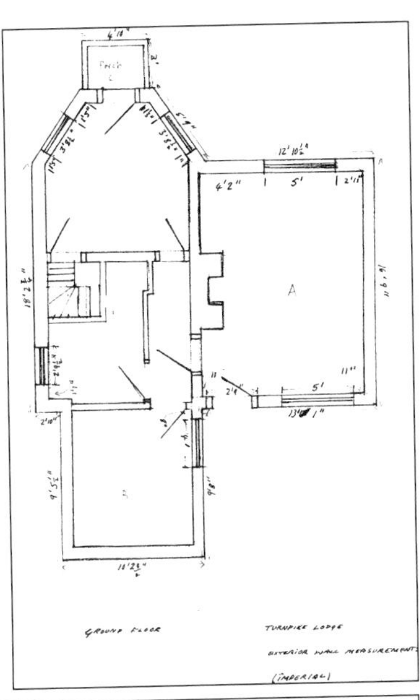

It is not certain when the toll house was built but there seems to have been a building on the site since at least 1820. The two-storey house was brick-built with a projecting wing towards the road. Later additions included an extension to the west and an enclosed porch at the front.

When the Trust was closed in 1868 the toll house was sold to the Estcourt estate for £55. The site was then described as being bounded on the north side by a road leading out of the Devizes

and Salisbury turnpike road to the village of Potterne; on the east by the last mentioned turnpike; and on all other sides by land belonging to Thomas Estcourt. The house was sold again in 1899. At some stage it was occupied by Fred Pottenger, superintendent of the Devizes cemetery and the final owner was Mr. Nigel Grist, a scrapyard proprietor. An application in 1980 to demolish the house was unsuccessful but in 1983 a fire, probably started by a vagrant, gutted the building and it was subsequently demolished.
TM(Devizes) WRO A1/205/7 WBR B502

Salisbury (Fisherton Anger)
Wilton Roads 1760-1870

SU 138 304 Fisherton Street, close to St Paul's Church and Wilton Road roundabout.

A toll house must have existed here from at least the late 18th century. The minutes of the Trust refer to the addition of a garden and to repairs in 1822. In 1829 it was decided to build a new toll house on the site of the existing one. John Peniston, the Salisbury architect, produced three sketch designs (two are reproduced below) but none of these was accepted. The actual building was undertaken by John Barnden for £387 7s. although later alterations were made

to the specifications which increased the cost by £15. On the closure of the turnpike in 1870, the toll house was demolished and the materials sold at auction. These materials were then used to build a house in Stratford Road which now houses the Avon Lodge Veterinary practice. The actual site was bought by the County (i.e. through the Quarter Sessions) for £130 to add to the land belonging to Fisherton Gaol. The abolition of the Fisherton Gate and the tolls was celebrated by the Salisbury Promenade Band playing a selection of music on a platform erected in a field belonging to the gaol.

There was also a weighing engine at Fisherton Bridge. In 1828 the Trustees ordered that the house adjoining the weighing engine at Fisherton Bridge be re-built and enlarged. This probably refers to the small house or booth which was normally attached to a weighbridge. The weighing house was to have a notice board advising that 'all and every wagon or carriage which shall come within 100 yards of such engine shall be weighed together with the loading thereof'. There is a further reference in 1830 to alterations to the engine house to improve the path for foot passengers. Two years later the Trustees were considering whether to repair or re-build the weighbridge.
TM(Wilton) WRO 451/74(xxxviii) DG(7Apr70)

Seend (Inmarsh)
Westbury Roads 1757-1872

ST 943 603 On the unclassified road from Seend to Lavington about half a mile south of the junction with the main A361 Trowbridge to Devizes road.

This is a brick two-storey building under a stone tile roof. It has had extensive modern extensions to the east. There is an old doorway facing the road; alongside it is a window with a wooden shutter.

Semington (The Ragged Smock)
Trowbridge Roads 1751-1870

ST 897 602 On A 350 Westbury to Melksham road on the north west side of the present Semington roundabout.

A turnpike gate appears on this site on the 1820 map. It probably ceased to be used as a toll house some time before the closure of the turnpike in 1870. It was then sold for £38 to John Lowell, carpenter, of Semington and was described as 'a house and garden situate near a place called the Ragged Smock in the tithing of Semington, formerly used as a toll house and now and for many years past in the occupation of the said John Lowell.'
WRO A1/205/18

South Newton (Stapleford)
Wilton Roads 1760-1870

SU 072 370 On the A36 road from Salisbury to Warminster at the sharp bend at Stapleford.

Early maps show a turnpike gate near the sharp bend on the A 36 road at Stapleford. The only other evidence is from a deed of 1870 on the closure of the turnpike when the trust sold a small piece of land to the Earl of Pembroke. It was described as being at Little Wishford and on which the Stapleford toll house 'has for many years stood but which has been or is about to be pulled down.' The plot was bounded on the south west by the turnpike road to Salisbury for a length of 55 feet; on the south east by the road leading from the turnpike to Winterbourne Stoke for a length of 66 feet; and on the north by the road connecting the other two roads for a length of 40 feet.
WRO A1/205/8

Southwick (Poleshole)
Trowbridge Roads 1751-1870

ST 833 550 On A 361 Trowbridge to Frome road in the centre of Southwick.

On the closure of the turnpike in 1870 the toll house with its garden was sold for £45 10s to Thomas Miller of Barrow Court, Barrow Gurney.
WRO A1/205/18

Swindon

Swindon was served by a number of turnpike roads including the Beckhampton Roads, the Swindon, Marlborough and Everleigh Road and the Swindon, Calne and Cricklade Road. Toll houses seem to have established along these roads on the outskirts of the town. Almost inevitably with the expansion of such a large town, the old toll houses and all traces of them have disappeared.

Our evidence for them is almost exclusively based on the series of drawings done by S.Adye about 1909 which were published with some comments in *A Swindon Retrospect* (1931) by Frederick Large. These show a series of very modest, single-storey thatched toll houses, all very similar in design. However, the ones at Coate Road and Stratton Road were rather more substantial being two-storeys of brick or stone under a tiled roof.

Large records that the toll house in Regent Street was opposite the Rifleman's Arms; it was left standing for many years and was used as a lock-up shop. He describes the area around Westcott Place as having a few mud cottages near the canal and a few houses at the Rushey Platt end with a turnpike gate and house at the end. The garden of the Rushey Platt toll house, of 1 rood and 8 perches, was sold in 1879 to William Dawson of Swindon for £50.

Large also says that from Bullin's Bridge on the station side of the town, not a house was to be seen save the Great Western Hotel Tap, the White House and a cottage near the line in the direction of the entrance to the Transfer where a

Adye's drawings of Swindon toll houses:

Stratton Road

Rushey Platt

Coate Road

Regent Street

Cricklade Road

Coate Road toll house

turnpike house and gates then stood. This is probably the toll house which was sold in 1876 to Charlton and Lougborough, trustees in a Chancery case. The other toll house sold to these trustees for a combined sum of £95 was described as being situated on the west side of the road at Eastcott Lane.

A little one-storey cottage stood under some high elm trees near the commencement of Manchester Road. The turnpike gates once stood there but were moved lower down in order to catch conveyances from the Gorse Hill district to the G.W.R. station.

The Stratton Road house was situated at Marshgate near the present industrial estate. The Trust minutes record the building of this house in 1793 by Mr. Wicks. At first a temporary house of deal board was constructed at a cost of £7 10s. This was followed by 'a turnpike house, a substantial building of stone, slate, timber and all proper materials' costing £61.

TM(Lechlade, Swindon) WRO A1/205/15 WRO A1/205/16 Large(SwRetro)

Trowbridge (The Down, Islington)

Trowbridge Roads 1751-1870

ST 859 587 At the southern end of The Down nearly opposite Canal Road.

Listed Grade II 9/87 No 41, The Old Toll House

Built in the early 19th century, this thatched toll house is single storey with an attic. It has an octagonal shaped front with a verandah supported on nine posts. The front door is pointed in the gothic style. Although the turnpike did not close until 1870, the toll house was sold in 1860 to Moses Barratt of Trowbridge, a clothworker, for £75.
LB WRO A1/205/18

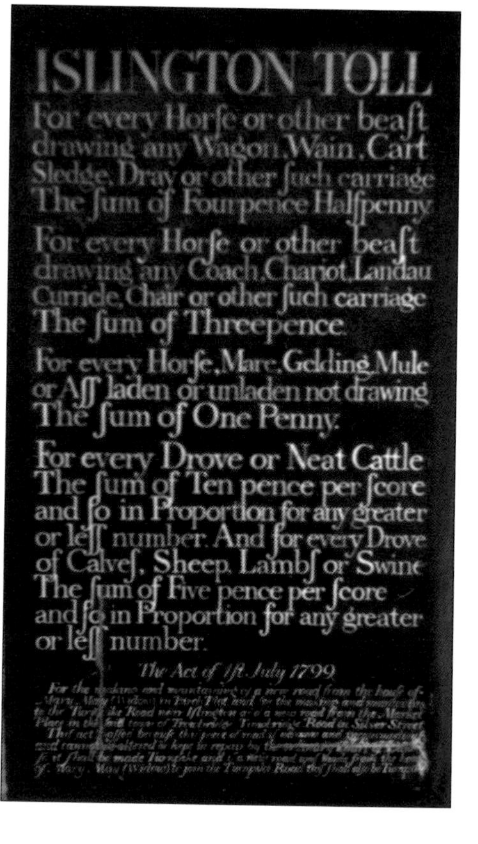

Trowbridge (PolebarnRoad)

Trowbridge Roads 1751-1870

ST 860 578 In Polebarn Road leading from Trowbridge to Steeple Ashton.

The original toll house was on the west side of Polebarn Road but it was replaced in 1840. The new toll house was a very substantial building and typical of the houses built by the Trowbridge Trust. They were later criticised for the extravagance of their buildings. The house remained as a private dwelling until it was demolished to make way for road improvements in the 1960s.

Marshman (Trowbridge)

Trowbridge (Sea Corner)

Trowbridge Roads 1751-1870

ST 862 596 In Trowbridge on the south side of Horse Road at its junction with Wyke Road.

The date of the original toll house is not known but, as it does not appear on the early maps, it was probably built about 1840 when other toll houses in Trowbridge were replaced. On the closure of the turnpike the house was sold to Richard Long of Rood Ashton.

WRO A1/205/18

Trowbridge (Stallard)
Trowbridge Roads 1751-1870

ST 851 577 Situated at the junction of the roads to Bradford-on-Avon (A363) and Radstock (A366)

This was a substantial two-storey building commanding an important junction on the west side of Trowbridge. On the closure of the turnpike in 1870 the house with a stable was sold to John Foley an auctioneer of Trowbridge for £270. It was demolished to make way for road improvements. There is also a reference in 1870 to a weighing engine being associated with this gate.

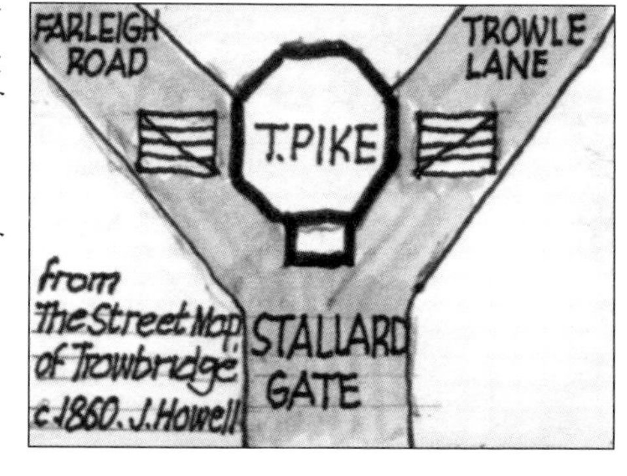

WRO G15/150/3 WRO A1/205/18 TNW Ad(1Oct70)

Trowbridge (Studley)

Trowbridge Roads 1751-1870

In their petition to the House of Commons committee in 1870, the complainants drew attention to the over-elaborate toll houses built by the Trust. They referred to one at Studley as being 'castellated'. When the Trust was closed in 1870, the sale of the property included the building materials of the gate and toll house by the Barracks which were situated at Studley.
TNW Ad(8May69) TNW Ad(1Oct70)

Upton Lovell

Wilton Roads 1760-1870

ST 947 412 Situated at Upton Lovell on the A36 Warminster to Salisbury road.

The stone cottage is single storey to the front with two storeys to the rear. There is a projecting central bay with a porch flanked by two light mullion windows with drip mouldings. The original stone porch with clock over the doorway was replaced in the 1960s but the stone footings remain. Opposite is the weighing house, a little stone booth with gothic doorway and single light window, now adapted to serve as a bus shelter.

The original toll house, described as being at the 'Heytesbury gate' was on the Knook/ Heytesbury boundary by the Chitterne turn, and was demolished in 1955. In 1836 it was decided to replace it with a new toll house at Upton Lovell. The new site was acquired from Mr.Everett in exchange for the old toll house and gardens at Knook plus a cash adjustment of £20. The plan for the new house was drawn up by Mr. Pinch of Bath and the building was undertaken by William Trapp of Warminster.

In the 1861 census the occupier of the toll house is John Gibbs, a cloth dresser, with his wife and family.

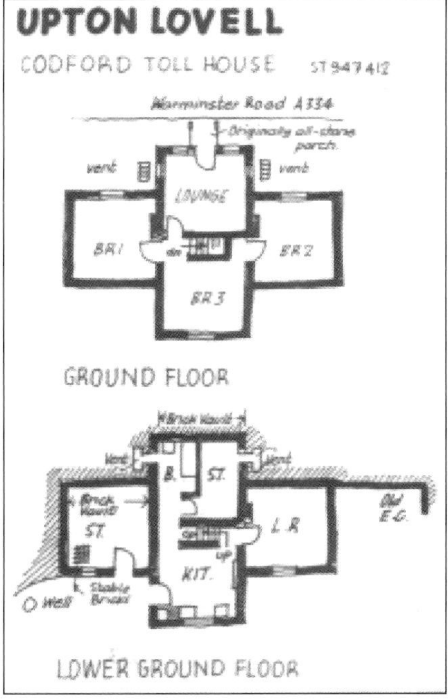

On the closure of the turnpike in 1870, the house was offered for sale first to Mr. Everett but he declined it and the house was then sold at auction. It was described as being 'very commodious, is a neat and modern erection in stone, slated and has the advantage of being very near a railway station and the factories at Upton Lovell. It was bought for £150 by James Goodfellow a shopkeeper of Codford.

A weighing engine was associated with this gate. In 1819 it was agreed to erect a new weighing engine at the Heytesbury gate on the principle of the model produced by Mr. Hopgood of Salisbury. Pigot's Directory of 1822 lists a George Hopgood, wheelwright. Problems must have arisen with the engine for in 1828 the Trust was looking to employ 'some competent person' to examine the weighing and advise whether it could be repaired or whether a new one should be built. In 1832 the Trust ordered a new weigh bridge at Heytesbury from Mr. Cockey at a cost of £65. It is probable that the weighing engine was moved to Upton Lovell when the new toll house was built there, for the weighing house appears to be of the same date and style.

TM(Wilton) WRO A1/205/8 WRO 628/35/4 Ginever, E D, Heytesbury (1974)

Upton Scudamore (Thoulstone)
Black Dog Roads 1751-1879

ST 841 480 On the A36 Warminster to Bath road, half a mile south of the A3098 crossroads.

On the closure of the turnpike the toll house with its outhouses was sold for £40 to Charles Phipps of Chalcot House. The Trust accounts refer to repairs being made to a weighing engine at Thoulestone in 1825/6 and again in 1826/7.
TM(Black Dog) WRO 540/4

Upton Scudamore (Rowe, Thoulstone)
Frome Roads (1756-1870)

ST 835 483 On the A3098 road from Westbury to Frome at the crossing with the A36 (Dead Maids)

On the closure of the turnpike in 1870 the toll house with its outbuildings and garden was sold for £40 to Isaac Lewis, a farmer from Upton Scudamore. Before 1880 it seems to have been acquired by Charles Phipps of Chalcot House whose grounds abutted the toll house. In that year he did an exchange with Elias Fowler, a labourer, of Holly Bush, Upton Scudamore. He gave Fowler the toll house plus £25 in exchange for his cottage. In 1892, a few years after Elias died, Phipps bought the toll house back from the Fowler family for £50.
WRO 540/122

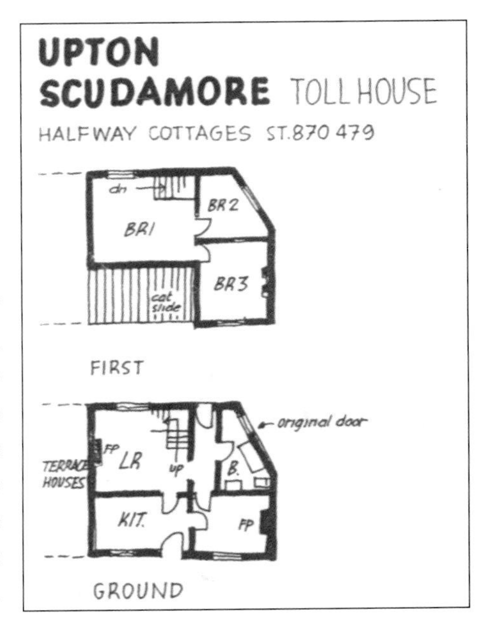

Upton Scudamore (Upton Scudamore)
Warminster Roads 1726-1871

ST 870 479 On the A350 Warminster to Westbury road at Halfway Cottages.

This house was clearly formed by adding a building to the end of an existing terrace of cottages. It is of two storeys and pentagonal in shape. The side was probably added later, the original door being in the side angled to the road. It has always been reputed to be a toll house and it has all the appearance of being one. Some doubt,

however, has been thrown on this as no building is marked on any of the early maps and there is no documentary evidence to clarify its origin and use.

Urchfont (Redhorn, Wedhampton)
Wilton Roads 1760-1870

SU 060 553 Situated on the old Devizes to Salisbury road where it crossed the Ridgeway.

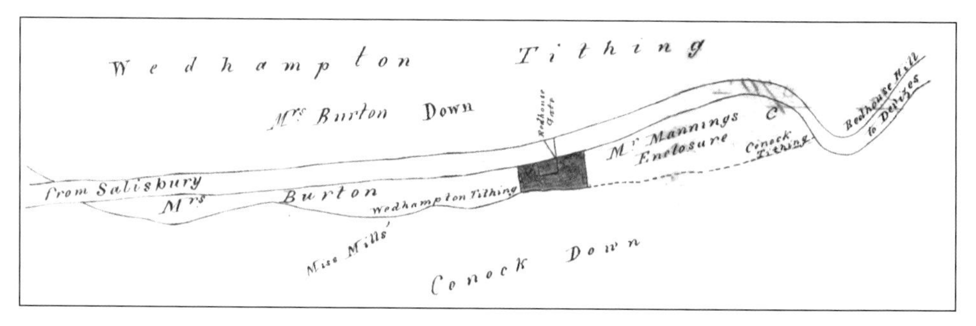

The Redhorn (or Redhouse) toll house was in an extremely remote spot in the middle of Conock Down. The Trust minutes for 1832 record that the toll house and the pond there should be repaired without delay. When the turnpike closed in 1870 the house and surrounding land, amounting to 22½ perches, was sold to Mrs Sarah Brown, a widow, of Bere Regis for £50 10s. It was then described as being bounded on the north by land lately downland but since enclosed by George Mannings of Wedhampton; on the east by land belonging to Miss Mills and occupied by Mr. Plummer; on the west by the turnpike road; and on the south by downland belonging to Mrs. Brown and occupied by Simon Taylor. *TM(Wilton) WRO A1/205/8*

Warminster (Boreham Road)
Warminster Roads 1726-1870

ST 883 446 Situated on the A36 towards Salisbury

Listed Grade II 4/170 Holly Lodge, 70, Boreham Road

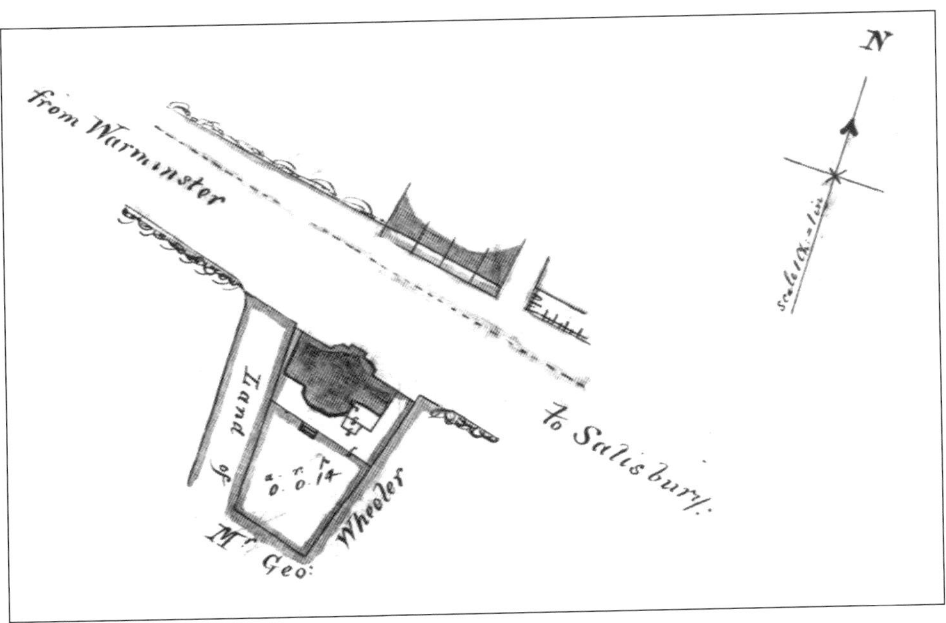

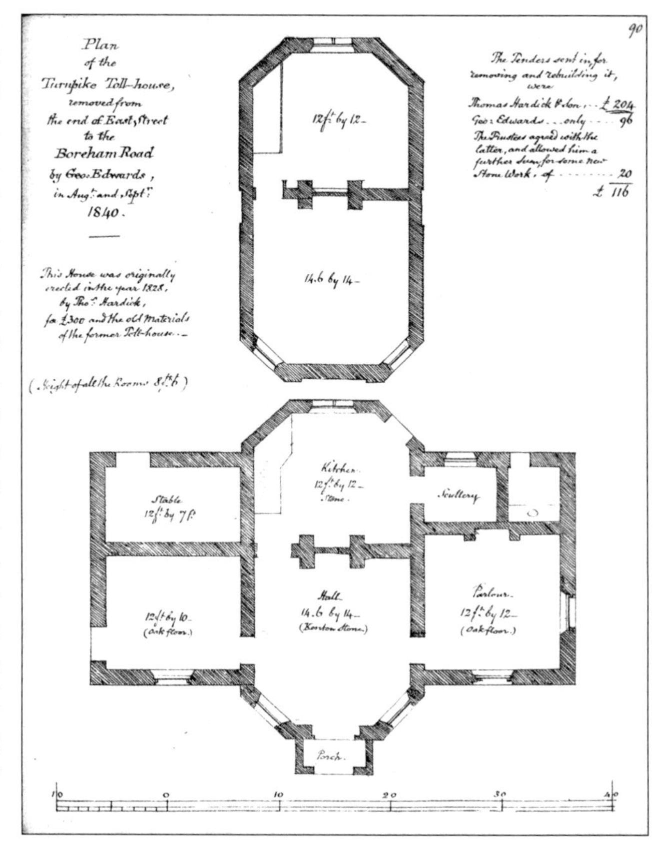

The first toll house, probably built in the 18th century, was demolished in 1828. The materials were then used to build a new house at the end of East Street. This was done by Thomas Hardick at a cost of £300. The house was moved again in 1840 to its present site in Boreham Road. It was re-erected by George Edwards, probably on the same plan, for £116. It is an imposing two-storey stone house with a hipped slate roof. The central section is angled although the projecting box porch was probably added later.

In the 1861 census, the turnpike gatekeepers living at the East Gate toll house, Boreham Road were William Davis and his wife, Harriet.

When the turnpike closed in 1870, the toll house (then known as the East End turnpike gate house) was sold for £170 to George Wheeler of Warminster, a nurseryman.

LB WRO A1/205/19 WRO 2735/1

Warminster (Bugley)

Frome Roads 1757-1870

ST 865 449 On A362 Warminster to Frome Road in Victoria Road.

The Frome Trust controlled the turnpike road (now A362) right into Warminster as far as the Bugley toll house which later became 32 Victoria Road. The building (illustrated overleaf) was demolished around 1980.

Houghton(Warminster)

Warminster (Bugley) toll house

Warminster (Copheap)
Warminster Roads 1726-1870

ST 876 456 In Warminster at the junction of Copheap Lane with the Portway.

The toll house was thatched and a relatively modest building. In 1927 it was described as a 'very unpretentious affair with few rooms and rapidly falling into ruin'. On the closure of the turnpike in 1870 the toll house was sold to the Marquis of Bath. It was demolished in 1959 to make way for road improvements.
WRO A1/205/19 Houghton (Warminster)

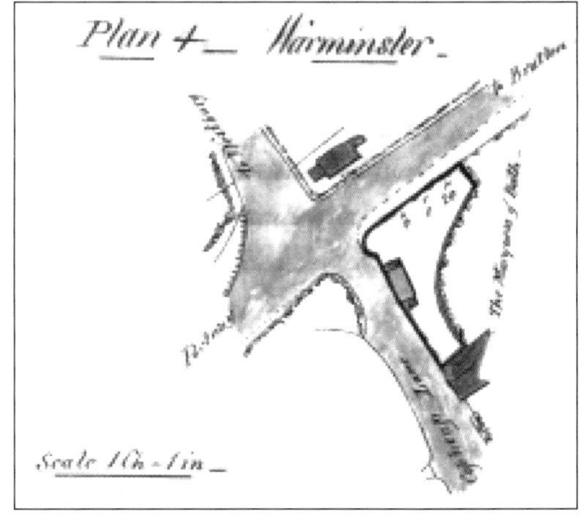

Warminster (Henfords Marsh)
Warminster Roads 1726-1870

ST 877 440 In Warminster at the junction of Smallbrook and Henfords Marsh.

Listed grade II 3/332 Turnpike Cottage, Smallbrook

The toll house was built in 1840 by Jacob Noyle at a cost of £97. It is thatched and of a picturesque design. Single storey, it is 'L' shape in plan with an octagonal projection to the west commanding a fork in the road. It is of local rubblework with brick quoins to dressings. There have been later extensions to the east and the central doorway is now blocked. On the closure of the turnpike

in 1870 the toll house was sold for £50 to Thomas Foreman.
LB WRO A1/205/19 Houghton (Warminster)

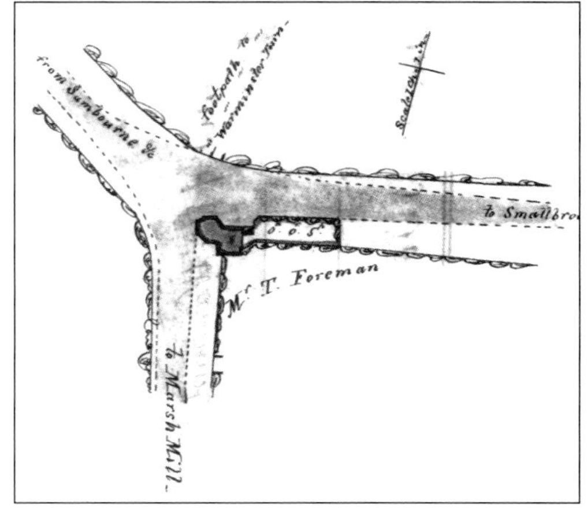

Warminster (Portway)
Warminster Roads 1726-1870

ST 875 455 In Warminster at the junction of the Portway with Portway Lane.

The toll house is quite substantial of brick with stone dressings and ornate chimneys. It was probably built in the mid 19th century. On the closure of the turnpike in 1870 the toll house was sold for £92 to Thomas Ponting, gentleman, of Warminster.
WRO A1/205/19

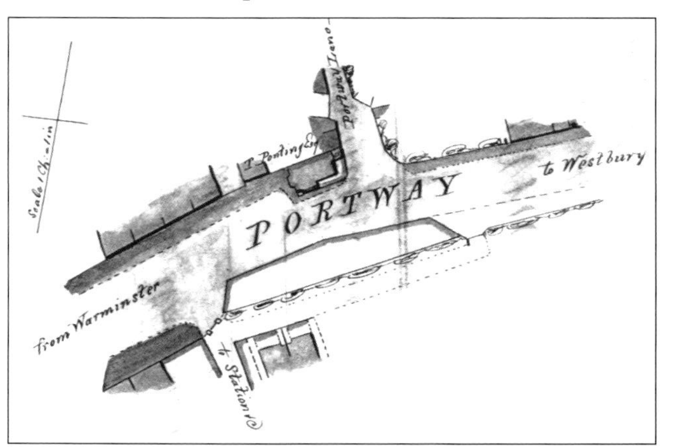

Warminster (Portway) toll house

Westbury (Warminster Road)
Westbury Roads 1757-1872

ST 868 502 On A350 Warminster Road at Chalford at the junction with the road to Dilton.

This relatively modest toll house was built in 1786. In April 1786 the Trustees decided to erect a gate 'at or near the Cross Ways at the upper end of Warminster Lane upon and across the turnpike road leading from Chalford to Madbrook'. They also erected a side gate on the road leading to Dilton. At the same time they purchased a site for the toll house which was built by John Elkins, carpenter, for £27 16s. Several later additions and alterations were made. In 1788 a shed for storing coal and wood was built. In 1789 an upper chamber was added to the toll house at a cost of £15 14s. 6d.

It is interesting that in 1791 the tolls of the Warminster Lane gate were leased to James Bartlett of Leigh, a labourer, at a yearly rent of £89 5s. It is possible that he also lived there as toll collector for he was allowed three guineas to dig a well for the use of the toll house. The toll house was demolished in 1960.
TM(Westbury)

Whiteparish (Earldoms)
Salisbury and Southampton Roads 1753-1870

SU 250 217 On A 36 Salisbury to Southampton road at Earldoms.

When the turnpike closed in 1870 the Earldoms toll house was advertised for sale in the *Salisbury Journal.* It was described as being brick built and tiled. It had a sitting room, a kitchen, two bedrooms and a wash house. It appears to have been sold for £26 to the Earl of Pembroke. The house is now a ruin. It must have measured about 30ft by 10ft, of 1½ or 2 storeys and with two chimneys.
WRO A1/205/13 SJ(3Apr70)

Wilton (Wilton)
Wilton Roads 1760-1870

SU 094 315 In West Street near St. John's Hospital.

The evidence for this toll house comes from the deed of sale when the turnpike closed in 1870. It was then sold for £45 to Mr. W. V. Moore, a general dealer. It was described as being bounded on the north east by the turnpike road; on the north west by the garden attached to St. John's hospital; on the south west by land belonging to the hospital and in the occupation of Messrs. Slow and Stone; on the south east by a road leading to the Netherwells.
WRO A1/205/8

Wingfield (Wingfield)
Trowbridge Roads 1751-1870

ST 822 567 On B3109 Bradford to Rode road at Wingfield at the junction with Chapel Lane.

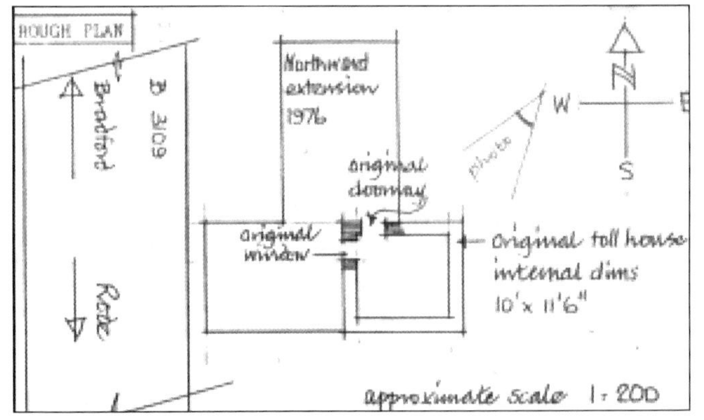

The original toll house was stone built and two storeys high but very small (13ft by 14½ft overall). This house is now largely submerged behind extensive later additions but the original arched entrance doorway is preserved as a feature in the room to the north. Although the Turnpike Trust was established in 1751, this section of the road was not turnpiked until 1799. The house could have been built before this as it was not unusual for a Trust to purchase an existing house rather than build a new one. When the turnpike closed in 1870, the toll house was sold for £68 to Charles Pickwick of Frankleigh, Bradford.
WRO A1/205/18

Winsley (Turleigh)
Bradford-on-Avon Roads 1751-1873

ST 807 605 On the unclassified road from Bradford-on-Avon to Turleigh on the eastern edge of the village.

Whereas the main turnpike roads had a series of gates with toll houses, the minor or side roads often had only a bar with a small booth or box for the protection of the toll collector. This photograph of the bar at Turleigh is a rare illustration of such a toll box. The Trust reorganised its gates in 1839 and this included putting a bar across 'Turley lane'. In the previous year the Trust had had specially made two toll boxes for other sites. These were to be 'of the proper dimensions . . . and made properly of Keanized timber'. This was timber saturated with Keyans patent solution, an early wood preservative. It is likely that the Turleigh box was similarly made. Rail-holes can still be seen in the stone wall on the north side of the road opposite where the original bar and box were sited.
TM(Bradford)

Winterslow (Lopcombe Corner)
Salisbury and Southampton Roads 1753-1870

There appear to have been two toll houses at Lopcombe (Lobcombe) Corner – one at the toll gate and, later, one at the toll bar. Plans (see overleaf) were submitted for the gate house in 1833 although it is not clear whether there had been an earlier toll house at the site. The more elaborate plan was rejected as too expensive and it is assumed that the simpler plan was accepted. In 1841 a toll house at the bar was built at a cost of £62 10s. 5d.

The minutes of the Trust record various repairs and alterations to the gate house. In 1845, for example, the staircase was repaired and in 1853 the outhouse was newly thatched. A more extensive repair was undertaken in 1862 when a new 'elm floor with proper sleepers' was installed. In 1866 the Trust agreed to make a new back door leading from the washhouse to the garden as previously

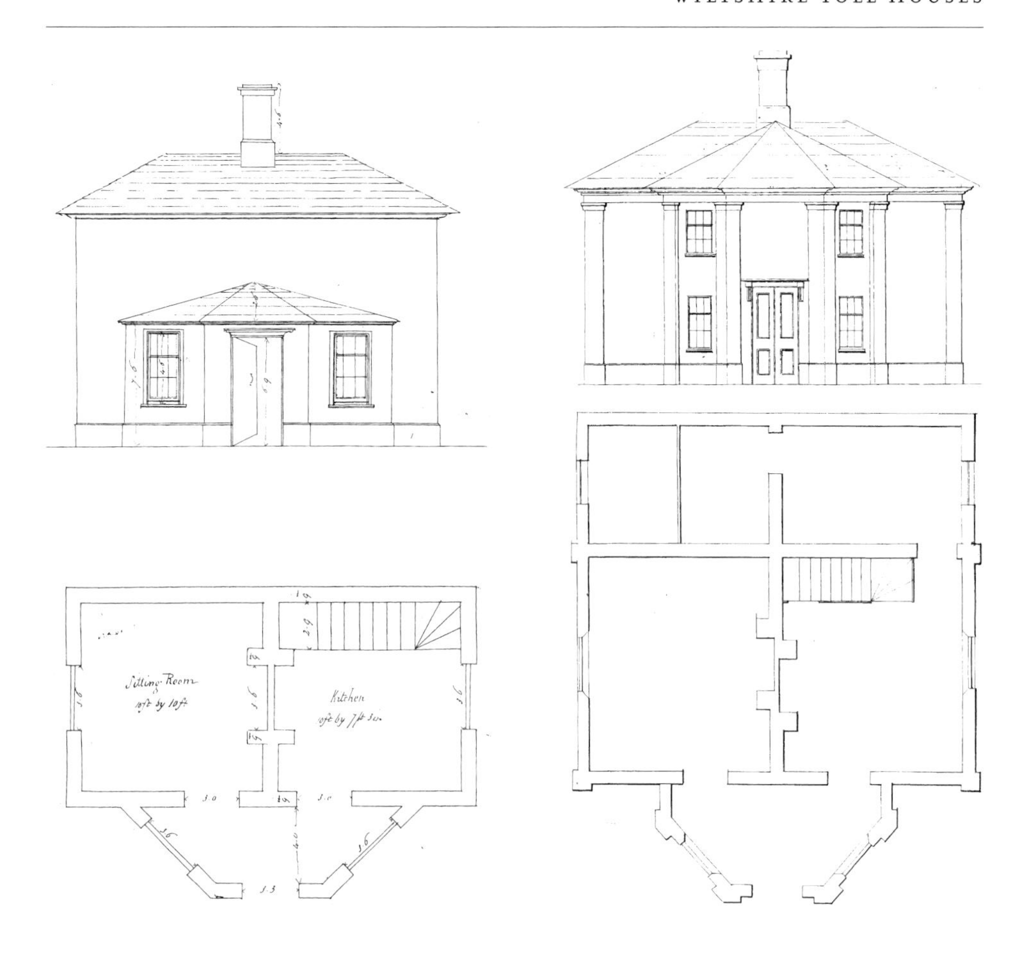

there was only the front door which had to serve for every purpose. (The existence of only the front door is consistent with the plan above.)

In 1870 the Lopcombe gate toll house was sold to the Ecclesiastical Commissioners for £125. It was then described as a toll house with a piece of land adjoining and containing eleven perches and numbered 245 on the tithe map for Milford. The toll bar house and garden (9 perches) was sold to Richard Blake. It was then said to have been lately occupied by John Smith, a shoemaker, as a servant (possibly toll collector) of William Mason of Frome who was the lessee of the tolls.

TM(Salisbury,Eling) WRO A1/205/13 WRO CC/Chap145/1-4 WRO 451/112

Worton (Cuckolds Green)

Westbury Roads 1757-1872

ST 983 575 On the road from Seend to Lavington at Worton, Cuckolds Green.

Turnpike Cottage. A toll house and gate are shown at the Cuckolds Green corner on the 1820 map. The house has been altered and extended in recent times with the bay windows added probably after 1960. The original house seems to be the west half, and the west gable end has old brickwork with a chimney and a window which looks directly along the road towards Worton. Unfortunately there is no further documentary evidence about its date or history.

Wroughton (Wharf Road)
Beckhampton Roads 1742-1870

SU 138 802 On the A361 Devizes to Swindon road on the south side of Wroughton.

There may have been an earlier toll house in Wroughton but in 1857 the Trust erected a new gate with side bar and toll house at the bottom of Wroughton hill near the road leading to the wharf. The inhabitants of Wroughton considered the gate an obnoxious eyesore in the middle of the village. In any case it proved to be of little value to the Trust for the local people opened up an old road to by-pass the gate. In 1859 they led a deputation to the Trust asking that the gate be moved further up the hill. It was eventually agreed that the gate and house be moved to a site 'at or near the wall of the Vicarage garden'. The toll house was taken down and the materials used to build the new house. For this concession the inhabitants had to pay £20 and, at their own expense, haul 'the several materials composing the present turnpike house' to the new site. The leader of

the movement against the toll gate had been Mr. Edward Watts and the village showed its gratitude to him by presenting him with a silver flagon costing £20 and large enough to hold two bottles of wine. It was inscribed 'Presented to Mr. Edward Watts for his spirited exertions in opposing the erection of a turnpike gate in the centre of the village of Wroughton A.D. 1858'. In 1870 on the dissolution of the turnpike, the Governors of Charterhouse agreed to buy the toll house for £55 but the sale fell through when they failed to get the approval of the Charity Commission. The toll house was then demolished and the materials sold to Captain Pavey for £20.
TM(Beckhampton) WRO A1/205/3 WRO 1171/Box 5(5b) SA(21Jun58)

Wroughton (Black Horse)
Swindon, Marlborough and Everleigh Road 1761-1875

SU 150 820 On the A361 Devizes to Swindon road to the north of Wroughton, now in a cul-de-sac near the M4 bridge.

This toll house was a modest one-storey building, square in plan, with a pyramidal room and central chimney stack. In recent years it has been much altered. On the closure of the turnpike, the toll house and garden were sold to Ambrose Goddard for £55.
WRO A1/205/17

Wylye (Wylye)
Amesbury Roads 1761-1871

SU 004 375 on the old A303 on the western edge of Wylye.

The Wylye toll house is a very modest one and similar in design to the Trust's toll houses at West Amesbury and Countess. It is not certain when it was built but the minutes of the Trust 1802-4 refer to a number of repairs and improvements – thatching, repairing a window and installing a stove. On the closure of the turnpike in 1871, the toll house was sold to Rev. Sidney Meade, rector of Wylye. It may have ceased to be a toll house some years before this as the deed refers to the house in 1871 having been already let to Rev. Meade on a yearly tenancy and, before that, to Rev. Joseph Stockwell then deceased.

There was another toll house to the north east of Wylye at Deptford (SU 012 383). The Trust minutes refer to various repairs being undertaken in 1806 but the toll house does not seem to have still been in the possession of the Trust in 1871.

TM(Amesbury) WRO 776/1083 Chandler(Amesbury)

References

General

LB: Listed building reports.
WBR: Wiltshire Buildings Record
WRO: Wiltshire and Swindon Record Office.

Books

Chandler(Amesbury): John Chandler *The Amesbury Turnpike Trust* (S. Wilts Industrial Arch. Soc. 1979)
Houghton(Warminster): Andrew Houghton *Before the Warminster Bypass* (Warminster History Society 1988)
Large(SwRetro): F. Large *Swindon Retrospect* (1931)
Marshman(Trowbridge): M. Marshman *Trowbridge in Old Photographs*
MHA(Melksham): Melksham Hist. Assoc *Around Melksham in Old Photographs*
Sp(Lidd): Sidney Palmer *Notes on Liddington*
VCH: *Victoria County History (Wiltshire)*
WRS: *Wiltshire Record Society*

Newspapers

DG: *Devizes and Wiltshire Gazette*
SA: *Swindon Advertiser*
SJ: *Salisbury Journal*
TAdv: *Trowbridge Advertiser*
TC: *Trowbridge Chronicle*
TNWAd: *Trowbridge and North Wilts Advertiser*
WT: *Wiltshire Times*

TM: Turnpike Trust minutes, accounts and papers: (WRO)

Amesbury	377/3,4
Beckhampton	1371/1,1a,2
Black Dog	628/41/13
Box, Seend	519/1
Bradford	G13/990/24,25,26
Calne	G18/990/1
Calne and Devizes	1171/Box5
Chippenham	542/3 1316/1,2
Christian Malford	542/4
Cirencester, W.Bassett	374/58

Devizes	1316/3
Lacock Blue Vein	542/1
Lechlade, Swindon	315/66
Sarum, Eling	1316/4,9
Swindon, Calne, Cricklade	1171/Box5
Westbury	1219/5,6
Wilton (Fisherton)	2491/1

Further Information

Although there is a considerable amount of literature on turnpikes in general, there is surprisingly little about toll houses in particular. Some recent publications about nearby counties are of help:

Patrick Taylor: *The Toll-houses of Cornwall* (Federation of Old Cornwall Societies 2001)
J.B.Bentley and B.J.Murless: *Somerset Roads; The Legacy of the Turnpikes Phase 1: Western Somerset; Phase 2: Eastern Somerset* (Somerset Industrial Archaeology Society 1985-7)
M.Tonkin: 'Herefordshire Toll Houses – Then and Now', *Trans. Woolhope Society*, Vol.48 (1996)

Bob Haynes collected a large amount of information about milestones in Wiltshire. Although this remains unpublished, his papers and photographs are deposited in the library of the Wiltshire Archaeological and Natural History Society, Devizes.

Source of Illustrations

Letters after the page numbers refer to the position on the page clockwise from top left.

Robert Haynes: front cover, pp. 1, 2, 3(a and b), 4(a), 8, 10, 11, 14, 15(a and b), 16(a), 20, 21(a), 25, 26(a and b), 27(b), 28(a and b), 29(a), 30(a and b), 31(b), 33(c), 36(b), 39, 44(b), 45(a and b), 46(b and c), 47(b), 48(a), 49, 50(a), 54, 56(a), 60(a and b), 62(b), 65, 70(b), 72(b), 73(b), 74(a), 75, 76(a), 84 (b and c), 87, 88(b)

Wiltshire Buildings Record: pp. 4(b), 5(a), 7, 17(b), 29(b), 33(d), 34, 38(b), 40, 41, 43(a), 44(a), 48(b), 51, 57(b), 58(a and b), 59, 61, 63(a and b), 74(b), 82(a), 84(a), 89(b)

Wiltshire and Swindon Record Office: pp. xvi, 3(c), 17(a), 19, 21(b), 23(b), 24(a), 31(a), 36(d), 42(b), 43(b), 47(a), 48(c), 50(b), 52(a), 55, 64(b), 73(a), 76(b), 77(b), 78, 80(b), 81(b and c), 86

Wiltshire Heritage Museum (library), Devizes: pp. 23(a), 35(a and b), 36(a)
Wiltshire County Council (Libraries and Heritage): frontispiece, pp. 16(b), 72(a), 85
English Heritage.NMR: pp. 9, 53
Victoria County History of Wiltshire: pp. 33(a), 36(a), 62(a)
Chippenham Museum: p. 27(a)
Cricklade Museum: pp. 32, 33(b)
Highworth History Society: p. 42(a and c)

Bradford on Avon – a pictorial record, H. Fassnidge and P. Maundrell, WLMS, 1983: p. 13
Chippenham and Lacock in Old Photographs, A. Wilson and M. Wilson, Alan Sutton, 1991: p. 24(b)
Devizes in Old Picture Postcards, P. Colman, European Library, 1983: p. 38(a)
Devizes in Focus, J. Girvan, Picton Publishing, 1989: p. 37
Devizes Gazette: p. xiii
The Story of Holt, No.3, the early years, K. Batchelor, Holt Magazine Editorial Board, 1974: p. 46(a)
Around Melksham in Old Photographs, Melksham and District Historical Association, Alan Sutton, 1989: pp. 5(b), 6, 56(b), 57(a)
A Swindon Retrospect 1855-1930, F. Large, S.R.Publishers, 1970: pp. 67(a and b), 68(a, b and c), 88(c)
Swindon in Old Photographs, Swindon Society, Alan Sutton, 1988: pp. 69, 88(a)
Trowbridge in Old Photographs, M. Marshman and M. Lansdown, Alan Sutton 1992: p. 71
Warminster in Old Photographs, D. Howell, Alan Sutton Publishing, 1989: p. 80(a)
Warminster Before the Bypass, A. Houghton, Warminster History Society, 1988: pp. 52(b), 77(a), 79(a and b), 81(a)
Westbury in Old Photographs, M. Randall, Alan Sutton, 1988: p. 82(b)

John Chandler: pp. 31(c), 64(a), 70(a), 89(a)
Mr. and Mrs. W.H.J. Fox, Trowbridge: p. 22(a and b)
Rosalind Pasmore: p. 83
Alan Thomsett: p.v

Some Useful Contacts

Wiltshire Buildings Record, Libraries and Heritage Headquarters, Bythesea Road, Trowbridge, Wiltshire BA14 8BS Telephone 01225 713740 (This is an independent organisation, open to the public on Tuesdays 9.00 am-5 pm. It contains information about more than 12,000 buildings in the county.)

Royal Institute of British Architects (for information on local architects), 66 Portland Place, London W1N 4AD Tel. 020-7580 5533 Website;- www.architecture.com

The Milestone Society, information from Terry Keegan, The Oxleys, Tenbury Road, Clows Top, Kidderminster, Worcs. DY14 9HE Website:- www.milestone-society.co.uk

Association for Industrial Archaeology, School of Archaeological Studies, University of Leicester, Leicester LE1 7RH. Tel. 0116 252 5337 Website:- www.industrial-archaeology.org.uk

Georgian Group, 6 Fitzroy Square, London W1P 6DX Tel 0207 387 1720 (for advice on the conservation and repair of 18th century buildings)

Victorian Society, 1 Priory Gardens, Bedford Park, London W4 1TT Tel. 0208 994 1019 (for advice on Victorian buildings) Website:- www.victorian-society.org.uk

District Council Conservation Officers (for advice on conservation and repair and on planning matters)

National Monuments Record Centre (for general records of buildings), Kemble Drive, Swindon SN2 2GZ Tel 01793 414700 Website:- www.english-heritage.org.uk

Wiltshire and Swindon Record Office, Bythesea Road, Trowbridge BA14 8BS Tel. 01225 713709 Website:- www.wiltshire.gov.uk

Wiltshire County Council, Local Studies Library, Bythesea Road, Trowbridge, Wiltshire BA14 8BS Tel. 01225 713732 Website:- www.wiltshire.gov.uk